Defoe Abbott Marx Hardy Machiavelli Montaigne Chesterton Cooper Emerson Haggard Joyce Austen
Melville Hugo Grimm
Stoker Christie Carroll Molière Eliot
Wilde Maupassant Byron Schiller
Garnett Einstein Fitzgerald Engels Smith Kafka
Goethe Hawthorne Hall
Cotton Dostoyevsky
Baum Kipling Doyle Willis
Henry Nietzsche
Leslie Dumas Flaubert Turgenev Balzac
Stockton Vatsyayana Crane
Burroughs Verne
Curtis Tocqueville Gogol Vinci
Homer Widger Tolstoy Whitman Busch
Darwin Thoreau
Potter Freud Zola Lawrence Twain Scott
Kant Jowett Stevenson Dickens Plato Harte
Andersen Hesse
London Descartes Burton
Poe Aristotle Voltaire Cervantes
Hale James Hastings Cooke
Bunner Shakespeare Irving
Richter Chekhov Chambers
Doré Dante Swift da Shaw Wodehouse Benedict Alcott
Pushkin
Newton

tredition®

Project Gutenberg

The Battle of Atlanta and Other Campaigns, Addresses, Etc.

Grenville Mellen Dodge

Imprint

This book is part of TREDITION CLASSICS

Author: Grenville Mellen Dodge
Cover design: Buchgut, Berlin – Germany

Publisher: tredition GmbH, Hamburg - Germany
ISBN: 978-3-8472-2006-0

www.tredition.com
www.tredition.de

MAJOR-GENERAL GRENVILLE M. DODGE

Commander
Department of the Missouri
1865.

THE
BATTLE OF ATLANTA

AND

OTHER CAMPAIGNS,
ADDRESSES, Etc.

BY

Major-General Grenville M. Dodge

COUNCIL BLUFFS, IOWA
THE MONARCH PRINTING COMPANY
1911

MAJOR-GENERAL SAMUEL R. CURTIS

Commander of the Army of the Southwest, in the Spring of 1861.

[Pg 9]

THE SOUTHWESTERN CAMPAIGN

The Southwest became prominent before the nation early in the war from the doubt existing as to the position of Missouri, which was saved by the energy and determination of Frank P. Blair and Colonel Nathaniel Lyon; the latter first capturing Camp Jackson, on May 10th, 1861. He then, picking up what force he could without waiting for them to be disciplined or drilled, marched rapidly against the Missouri State troops under Price, who were driven to the southwest through Springfield, where, being joined by the troops from Arkansas, under Colonel McCullough, they stood and fought the battle of Wilson's Creek. This would have been a great victory for the Union forces if Lyon had not divided his forces at the request of General Siegel and trusted the latter to carry out his plan of attack in the rear while Lyon attacked in the front. This General Siegel failed to do, leaving the field when the battle was half over, and allowing Lyon to fight it out alone. Even then, if Lyon had not been killed at the head of his Army while fighting the whole force of the enemy, it would have turned out to be a great victory for the Union forces, and would have held that country. The death of Lyon caused a return of his troops to Rolla and Sedalia, and opened up again the whole of Missouri to the Missouri State troops under General Price.

One of the notable facts of this battle of Wilson's Creek was that it was fought by young officers who ranked only as Captains and Lieutenants, all of whom afterwards became distinguished officers in the war—Schofield, Sturgis, Totten, DuBois, and Sweeny—and from the fact that in the first great battle of the Southwest one of the two commanders of Armies falling at the head of their forces in battle was killed here—General Lyon. The other was General McPherson, who fell at Atlanta.

Lyon pursued the tactics of Grant by attacking the enemy wherever to be found, and not taking into consideration the disparity of forces. The excitement caused by Lyon's campaigns induced [Pg 10] the Government to create the Western Department, and assign to it on July 25th, 1861, General John C. Fremont as its commander.

In August, 1861, I landed in St. Louis with my Regiment, the Fourth Iowa Infantry, and soon after was sent to Rolla, Mo., which was then the most important outpost, being the nearest to the enemy's Army. Soon after I reached there General Fremont commenced formulating his plans for the campaign in the South, and being the commander of that outpost I was in daily communication with him. There was a constant stream of reports coming from the enemy's lines that seemed to give great importance to their strength and their position, and I was continually ordered to send out scouts and troops to test the information. I invariably found it wrong and my telegrams will show my opinion of those reports.

Soon after arriving at Rolla I was placed in command of the post, and had quite a force under me, and was ordered to prepare to winter there.

The battle of Wilson's Creek was fought on August 10th, and soon thereafter General Price formed his plan of campaign to move north into north Missouri and endeavor to hold it by the recruits that he could obtain there. With from five to ten thousand men of the Missouri State Guards, General Price moved, and as he marched north in September his Army increased heavily in numbers and enthusiasm. The Federal forces were scattered all over Missouri— some eighty thousand in all. At least half of these could have been concentrated to operate against any force of the enemy, but they were all protecting towns, cities and railways and endeavoring to make Missouri loyal, while Price concentrated and moved where he pleased, until, on September 21, 1861, he captured Lexington, with some 3,000 or more prisoners. The movement of Price on Lexington and the defeat and capture of our forces there, forced Fremont to concentrate, and he moved with four Divisions, making an Army of 38,000, on Springfield, which he reached October 27th. Price was then far south of that place. Had our forces been concentrated to meet Price's Army we had enough to defeat him; but the moment Fremont commenced concentrating his four Divisions to act against him, Price moved back as fast as he had advanced, and did not stop until he was south of Springfield and near supports in Arkansas.

[Pg 11] General McCullough, in his letters from Springfield, Mo., August 24th, says that there were only 3,000 troops in Springfield and all the Arkansas troops had left the service. Price's total force was about 12,000 men, and on November 7th he reached and joined McCullough and suggested to General A. S. Johnston a campaign against St. Louis, offering to raise in Missouri and Arkansas a force of 25,000 men in such a campaign, and stated he should wait for Fremont at Pineville, Ark., believing in that rugged country he could defeat him.

While at Rolla I was ordered to send a force to take Salem, to the south of me, and I entrusted the command of the force to Colonel Greusel, of the Thirteenth Illinois Infantry. I issued to him the following instructions:

If the men who are away from home are in the rebel Army, or if their families cannot give a good account of them or their whereabouts, take their property or that portion of it worth taking; also their slaves. Be sure that they are aiding the enemy, then take all they have got.

When I wrote these instructions I had not considered for a moment what a row the order to take the slaves would cause. I simply treated them as other property. It was written innocently, but made a sensation I never dreamed of, and I have often since been quoted as one of the first to liberate and utilize the negro.

On the return of Lyon's Army to Rolla I was ordered by General Fremont to report at his headquarters in St. Louis. On my arrival in St. Louis I reported myself to his Adjutant, who was in the basement of the old home of Thomas A. Benton, on Choutau Avenue, but was unable to obtain an interview with the General. I showed my dispatch to his Adjutant-General, and waited there two days. I met any number of staff officers, and was handed about from one to another, never reaching or hearing from General Fremont. After remaining in St. Louis two days I considered it was my duty to return to my command, and left a note to the Adjutant stating that I had waited there two days for an interview with General Fremont, and had left for my command, and that if wanted would return to St. Louis again.

Evidently no communication was made to Fremont of my presence in the city or of my note, for soon after I arrived at Rolla I received a sharp note from him asking why I had not reported as ordered. I answered by wire that I had reported, had been unable to see him, and would report immediately again in St. Louis. I was determined to see him this time, and I, therefore, went directly [Pg 12] to Colonel Benton's house, and, taking a sealed envelope in my hand, marched right up the front steps, passed all the guards as though I belonged there, and went into his room and reported myself present. I there learned from him as much of his plans as he thought best to give me in regard to his movements, and obtained from him the information that Price's Army was not far from Rolla, and instructions to be on the alert. I supposed that my command at Rolla was to accompany his march to Springfield, and on my return to Rolla made every preparation to do so, but never received the order. Everything in the department was absolutely chaos. It was impossible to obtain provisions, accouterments, equipment, or anything else upon a proper requisition. Everything seemed to require an order from one of General Fremont's staff, and my own Regiment suffered a long time before I could get for it the necessary arms, clothing, equipment, etc.

While I was at Rolla the dispatch sent by the Government to General Curtis, to be forwarded to Fremont at Springfield, relieving him of the command, was brought by a staff officer to me with the request that I should see that the staff officer had an escort and went through promptly to Springfield. General Curtis, who was from my own state, wrote me a private note stating the importance of pushing this staff officer through. President Lincoln sent the order to General Curtis with this peculiar note:

Washington, October 24, 1861.

Brigadier-General S. R. Curtis:

My Dear Sir:—Herewith is a document, half letter, half order, which, wishing you to see but not to make public, I send unsealed. Please read it and then inclose it to the officer who may be in command of the Department of the West at the time it reaches you. I cannot know now whether Fremont or Hunter will then be in command. Yours truly,

A. Lincoln.

In a few days I received a letter from General Hunter, who had relieved General Fremont, instructing me that thereafter everything in the department must be carried on in accordance with the orders of the War Department and the Army Regulations, and I immediately saw a change for the better. I was soldier enough, although I had not had much experience then, to know that the methods being pursued under Fremont could bring nothing but disaster to the service. Every order was signed by somebody acting as a General, a Colonel, or something else, while in fact many of them had no rank whatever, and in looking over my own orders I do not know why I did not sign myself as an Acting General, [Pg 13] as those who succeeded me did. Even after General Halleck took command I noticed in the orders of General Hunter that he assigned persons to the command of a Brigade as Acting Brigadier-Generals instead of their rank as Colonel Commanding, etc.

I remained at Rolla until the return of the troops under General Hunter; and finally those commanded by Siegel, Asboth and Osterhaus were encamped at Rolla outside of the post and were reporting directly to the commanding officer of the department, while I as post commander reported directly to the same authority.

General Hunter as soon as he took command wired the War Department that there was no force of the enemy in his neighborhood, although orders had been given by Fremont a day or two before to march out and fight Price's Army. Hunter, therefore, in accordance with his orders from Washington, abandoned the pursuit, although with the force he had he could have driven Price and McCullough south of the Arkansas River, and probably have avoided the later campaign that ended in the Battle of Pea Ridge. Hunter moved his forces back to Rolla and Sedalia and sent 18,000 of his men to join General Grant in the campaigns up the Tennessee River.

This force at Rolla was mostly Germans, and the change of commanders from Fremont to Hunter, and later to Halleck, was unsatisfactory to them, though one of the officers, General Osterhaus, took no part in the feeling and sentiment that seemed to exist that for success it was necessary to have Fremont or Siegel in command, and my understanding was that the force at Rolla during the winter of 1861-62 was the nucleus of the force that was again to march to the

Southwest under the orders of General Halleck and to be commanded by General Siegel. General Halleck, when he assumed command of the department, in his letters to the War Department and his orders to the troops showed plainly his disgust at the condition of matters in that department. He wrote to the War Department:

One week's experience here is sufficient to prove that everything is in complete chaos. The most astounding orders and contracts for supplies of all kinds have been made, and large amounts purported to have been received, but there is nothing to show that they have ever been properly issued and they cannot now be found.

Of the condition of the troops he found in his department, he wrote:

[Pg 14] Some of these corps are not only organized in a way entirely contrary to law, but are by no means reliable, being mostly foreigners, and officered in many cases by foreign adventurers, or perhaps refugees from justice; and, having been tampered with by political partizans for political purposes, they constitute a very dangerous element to society as well as to the Army itself. Wherever they go they convert all Union men into bitter enemies. The men, if properly officered, would make good soldiers, but with their present officers they are little better than an armed mob.

They were not paid, had not been mustered into our service, and the commissions emanated from General Fremont, not from the State or Government.

General Halleck's plans evidently were to make a campaign against Price as soon as he could organize the forces concentrated at Rolla. Price's headquarters were at Springfield, and his northerly line was along the Osage Valley. His force was estimated anywhere from 10,000 to 30,000. As outposts General Halleck had Rolla, Jefferson City, and Sedalia. There was located at Rolla five or six thousand troops; at Sedalia and along that line about ten or twelve thousand, under General Pope, including Jeff C. Davis's Division; but these troops Halleck intended to send down the Mississippi and up the Tennessee.

General Pope in his letters to General Halleck urged that he be allowed to move on Price and destroy his Army, which he said he could do with his force. Rumors of Price's force and their movements were a constant terror and excitement throughout Missouri. The whole of northern Missouri was aroused by Price's proximity, and all the counties had recruiting officers from his Army enrolling and sending it recruits. The numbers of these recruiting officers and their small squads of recruits were magnified into thousands, and Price, when he sent a thousand men to Lexington for the purpose of holding that place and recruiting, brought orders from Halleck for a movement of all the troops to cut him off. The prompt movement of Halleck kept him from remaining there very long, but he was enabled to take about three thousand recruits from there without molestation from us.

Price's campaign as planned for the winter was to have General McCullough's Arkansas force, which was lying at Cross Timbers, near Elkhorn Tavern, and Van Buren in Arkansas, join him. Price complained bitterly of his inability to obtain any aid from McCullough, stating that if he could obtain it he could march into northern Missouri and hold the State, and recruit there an Army of Missourians; which, from my experience in the State, I have [Pg 15] no doubt he would have done if he could have moved there and held his position.

General Halleck's plan evidently was to move a body from Rolla directly on Springfield, with the intention of striking and defeating Price before Price could receive reinforcements, but Halleck had a great disinclination to move until he had organized the forces in the State of Missouri into Brigades and Divisions, had them properly mustered and officered, and had his staff departments so arranged that they could be depended upon to take care of any moving column. This disinclination of Halleck to move carried us on to the first of January.

In December General Siegel was given command of the troops at Rolla, and Captain Phil Sheridan was sent there as Quartermaster for that Army. His ability and foresight in organizing the transportation of an Army, feeding it, and fitting it for a campaign, was shown every day.

On December 26th General Halleck assigned General S. R. Curtis to the command of the District of Southwest Missouri. This included the forces under Siegel at Rolla, and caused very severe comments from them. From the letters of Halleck, written at the time and afterwards, this placing of Siegel under Curtis was caused by the letters and opinions — in fact, the denunciations — of Siegel made by Captains Schofield, Totten, and Sturgis, when with Lyon in the Wilson's Creek campaign. Evidently Halleck lost all faith in Siegel as commander of the Southwestern Army, and therefore assigned Brigadier-General Samuel R. Curtis, who had been stationed at St. Louis, to the command. But General Siegel was still left in command of two Divisions of the troops near Rolla, which was a great mistake.

As soon as General Curtis assumed command General Halleck commenced urging him to move to the south on Springfield, agreeing to send to him Colonel Jeff C. Davis's Division to join him before reaching Springfield, which Division was about 5,000 strong, and was with Pope on the Lamine River line. Curtis hesitated, and did not feel secure with the forces he had, although Halleck did not believe Price would stand for a fight, or that Curtis would need Jeff C. Davis's Division.

The Army of the Southwest, about seven thousand strong, was organized at Rolla, and moved from there January 14th, towards Springfield, halting at Lebanon. From Lebanon it moved on to [Pg 16] Marshfield, where Colonel Jeff C. Davis, with his Division, joined it. Great preparations were made there for the attack upon Price, and we moved out of Marshfield prepared for battle, General Siegel commanding the First and Second Divisions, one under General Osterhaus and the other under General Asboth. General Jeff C. Davis, from General Pope's Army, commanded the Third Division, and Colonel Eugene A. Carr the Fourth Division, a Brigade of which I commanded.

When within about three miles of Springfield we received orders to attack that town the next morning, and moved at midnight. All the reports we received were that Price was in Springfield ready for battle. I had the extreme left, and put out my skirmishers soon after midnight, supposing, of course, that I was in front of the enemy, although I had seen nothing of them. In the darkness I lost track of the company of the Fourth Iowa, who were the skirmishers of my Brigade, and was greatly worried at the fact, but at daylight I met them on the road mounted upon horses and dressed in all kinds of costumes. The officer in command, who was an enterprising one, had started his skirmish-line, and, not meeting any enemy, had pushed right into Springfield, which he found evacuated except for a rear guard and a number of horses. They mounted the horses and rode back to us. All this time our extreme right, under Siegel, was using its artillery upon the town, not knowing that the enemy had gone.

General Curtis, in his order of battle, instructed Captain Sheridan to line up his transportation in the rear of the line of battle, so that it could be used as a defensive obstruction for the troops to fall back to, provided they met any check or were driven back. Captain Sheridan looked on this order as a very singular one, and says that he could, in his imagination, if anything happened our army, see his transportation flying over that rough country, knowing that his mule-drivers would be the first to run, most likely from a false report, not even waiting for an attack. While this order at the time caused no comment, it now, after our long experience, looks very ridiculous, though not more so than many others, we received at the beginning of the war.

It was not long before we were all on the march through and beyond Springfield, Price and his Army being in full retreat, with a force, so far as we could learn, of about ten thousand men. We followed him as rapidly as possible, he leaving a strong [Pg 17] rear guard under Colonel Little to stop us at every stream. General Siegel had urged upon General Curtis a detour by his two Divisions to head off Price or stop him, so that he could attack him in front while we attacked his rear. Curtis had acceded to this. I had the advance following up Price, and endeavored to hold him, while Siegel moved by another road, expecting to catch him in flank or get ahead of him.

I remember that about noon of each day at some good defensive point, generally across a creek with a wide, open valley, Price would open out with his artillery and cavalry and act as though he intended to give battle. Our cavalry would fall back to give way to our infantry, and we would go into line, put out our skirmishers, and lose half a day, and as night came on Price would get out without our accomplishing anything. I remember distinctly that my Regiment would go into line, strip themselves, and throw down the chickens, potatoes, apples, and other eatables they had foraged and taken during the day, and as they would go forward the troops in our rear would come up and gobble what they had dropped. About the third time the Regiment went into line I noticed the boys had left nothing but their knapsacks, and were holding on to their chickens and provisions. One of the boys saw me looking at them, and thinking I was going to order them to drop what they had in their hands or on their backs, he appealed to me, saying, "Colonel, we have fed that damned Thirty-sixth Illinois Infantry every day and left ourselves without any supper. They put up this game that is going on to get our chickens. There ain't any Price on that side of the river, and they can't fool us any longer if they do you."

At Cane Creek, Flat Creek, Sugar Creek, etc., we had pretty sharp skirmishes. I soon discovered the plan of Price. It was to leave a strong rear-guard and make a great show while his trains and the rest of his Army were pushing to the South as fast as possible; so as soon as I saw him stop I went at him head-on with the cavalry and infantry, not even waiting to deploy more than a Regiment. Price's men would line the road and get one or two volleys at us and then slip off into the woods before we could deploy or return their fire. They did not get hurt much, but we did; but at the same time it broke up his game of holding us back, and we kept close on to his rear. For two or three days we were looking for Siegel to get in ahead and check Price, when to our astonishment [Pg 18] a report came from our rear that he had turned his column in on our road some eight miles behind us, and there was a general howl from the force that had been pounding away at Price's rear.

Finally we pushed Price back to Fayetteville, Ark., where we landed during the month of February, and where we were halted by General Halleck's orders, who stated that he would relieve our front of the enemy by his movements with the rest of his forces through Southeast Missouri, down the Mississippi, and up the Tennessee.

While Price was laying at Springfield, in December, he communicated with the Confederate Government, and changed all his Missouri State force as far as practicable into Confederate troops. He also complained to the Government, and to General Polk, who commanded at Columbus, Ky., of the impossibility of obtaining the co-operation of the Confederate forces west of the Mississippi River. From the representations of Polk and Price, the Confederate Government organized all the country west of the Mississippi River into a department known as the Trans-Mississippi District, and placed it under the command of General Earl Van Dorn, who assumed command early in February, 1862. As soon as he assumed command General Van Dorn prepared to make an aggressive campaign, using all his forces in Arkansas and those under Price, estimating that they would reach 30,000 troops. His plan was to move his forces directly from Arkansas northward, west of Iron Mountain, by way of Salem, while Price moved from Springfield directly east and joined his column by way of Salem and Rolla, thence the combined column to move directly on St. Louis, Van Dorn calculating that he could strike and capture St. Louis before Halleck could concentrate his troops or obtain any knowledge of his movements that would enable him to defeat him before reaching St. Louis. Van Dorn expected to make this move in February, and his plans and the energy with which he executed them and concentrated his troops shows him to have been an officer of ability and great energy. General Halleck's prompt movement of General Curtis's army from Rolla southwest in January, thus driving Price out of Springfield, compelled Van Dorn to change his plans, and instead of moving towards St. Louis he moved his troops by Van Buren and the Boston Mountains, making a junction with Price's force in the Boston Mountains below Fayetteville, and while General Curtis's [Pg 19] Army was laying at Cross Hollows, evidently in full security, thinking his campaign was over and expecting Price and Van Dorn to be drawn away from his front by the movement down the Mississippi. General Curtis was obliged to scatter his forces in that destitute country over a wide expanse so as to obtain food and forage. Van Dorn, without our having any knowledge of the fact, marched over the Boston Mountains, and it was March 3d before General Curtis was aware that Van Dorn was almost in his front and on his flank. The Union refugees flying before Van Dorn's movement gave us the first reliable notice of the new combination and the new movement. General Curtis immediately sent out orders, and, by marching all night, during heavy snows and severe cold weather, was able to concentrate most of his force on Sugar Creek, near Bentonville. General Siegel and his force did not move promptly, as ordered by Curtis, and was almost cut off before reaching Bentonville. He had to cut his way through a portion of Van Dorn's Cavalry, which he was able to do without much loss, and our line was formed on the north side of Sugar Creek, facing to the south, — a strong position, — expecting to receive Van Dorn's attack on the main telegraph road from Fayetteville to Springfield. We were on a plateau with a broad open valley in our front. In the rear of us was what was known as the Cross Timbers, a deep gorge. To the west of us was much open ground, over which was a road parallel to the main road, passing down what was known as Little Cross Timbers, and entering the Springfield and Fayetteville road about midway between Elkhorn Tavern and Cassville, some four miles in our rear.

While I was in command at Rolla I had organized by details from the Twenty-fourth and Twenty-fifth Missouri Regiments a Corps of scouts who lived in Northern Arkansas and Southern Missouri and were thoroughly acquainted with that country. During the day of the 6th of March, while Siegel was joining us and we were preparing for the battle, some of these scouts came to me and told me that Van Dorn proposed to move to our rear by this Little Cross Timber road. About 4 o'clock in the afternoon I went to General Curtis and reported these facts to him, and also told him of this road and of the feasibility of blockading it, supposing, of course, he would send some of the troops on his extreme right to do it; but he turned to me and said: "You take a portion of your command and go there and blockade the road."

[Pg 20] It was after dark before I could reach the Little Cross Timbers, as I had to march infantry to the place, which was quite a distance away from where we were. I took six companies of the Fourth Iowa Infantry and one company of the Third Illinois Cavalry and marched to carry out this order. In the dark two of my companies crossed the road and got lost, while with the other five I got into Cross Timbers Hollows and spent about three hours felling trees all through the gorge, and only left when my cavalry reported the movement of Van Dorn's Army coming down the road. I returned to my camp supposing my two companies had been cut off, but upon discovering that the enemy were coming down the road they managed to get back across it and reached the camp.

I reported immediately to General Curtis's headquarters, and informed him that Van Dorn's Army was moving down that road to his rear. He did not believe it, and thought that I had mistaken some of his cavalry for Van Dorn's Army. There were no pickets out on our right flank, and I so reported to General Curtis, but evidently my report made no impression upon him, and I returned to camp.

Early on the morning of the 7th of March I received a request from General Curtis to report at a schoolhouse that was on the main Fayetteville road a half mile north of Sugar Creek, where I met all the commanders of Divisions, and, I think, some of the Brigade commanders, and where a council of war was being held as to the policy that was to be pursued. I was so confident that Van Dorn was in our rear that when I went to this council I took my Brigade and halted it on the road near where the council was to be held. Generals Siegel, Asboth, and a majority of the officers present, advised that we should fall back to Cassville towards Springfield, and not give battle there, but Colonel Jeff C. Davis and myself protested, and I stated that I believed a portion of Van Dorn's force was then in our rear. The rear of Curtis's Army was in a great deal of confusion; its trains were stretched out on the Fayetteville road and the ground that we were upon was wooded and not very defensible for a battle, unless they attacked us on the Sugar Creek front.

While we were in this council, about 8:30 a. m., scattered firing commenced in our rear near the Elkhorn Tavern, and General Curtis inquired what it was, and asked what troops those were that [Pg 21] were out upon the road. I answered that they were mine, and he ordered Colonel Carr to immediately send me to the Elkhorn Tavern and ascertain what the firing meant.

Colonel Carr evidently was of the same opinion as myself, and accompanied me as I moved as rapidly as possible to the Elkhorn Tavern, where we went without being deployed right into battle; in fact, right into the enemy's skirmishers. The fact is, the first notice I had that the battle was on was when a shell fell among my drummers and fifers, who were at the head of my Regiment, and killed and demoralized them, so that we heard no more of drumming and fifing that day. I immediately deployed a company of the Fourth Iowa, which had been thoroughly drilled as skirmishers, and pushed forward toward the White River road, seeing some teams of the enemy passing that way with forage, and I pushed down the slopes of the Cross Timber Hollows nearly a mile before I developed the enemy in force.

The firing of the artillery and the sharp skirmish firing of my movement satisfied Colonel Carr that the enemy was in force in my front, and he immediately sent back word for his other Brigade, Commanded by Colonel Vandever, of the Ninth Iowa Infantry, to come to the rear, now our front. They had hardly reached the Elkhorn Tavern and deployed into line before Price's whole Army moved in on us in line of battle and disabled two of our batteries. The fighting on this front, with only Carr's two Brigades in line, the strength of both not exceeding three thousand men, was kept up continuously all day, until dark, with varying success.

As soon as I saw, near the middle of the day, the formation of the enemy, I knew that I could not hold the extended line we were covering, and I commenced drawing in my right and closing on Vandever until I backed down through an open field that had been cleared, and where the logs had been hauled to the lower edge of the slope to make a fence. Behind these logs I placed my Brigade and fought all the afternoon, with the enemy sometimes around both flanks and sometimes in my rear.

Colonel Vandever held his line at the Elkhorn Tavern in the edge of thick timber on the main Fayetteville road until late in the afternoon, fighting desperately, when the enemy, taking advantage of the timber as a blind, by largely superior numbers, drove him back across an open field to a line of woods in his rear and in my rear, which he successfully held. I was not aware of his movement [Pg 22] until the fire in that direction slackened, and I sent out my adjutant, Lieutenant James A. Williamson (afterwards a Brevet Major-General), who returned and reported that the enemy were in possession of that field; in fact, he ran right into them and received their fire, but got back to me safely. It was then nearly dark. The fire on my front had slackened, and my Brigade was almost entirely out of ammunition. I immediately ordered them to form in column and led them right out from the right, moving in the direction where Vandever's Brigade had formed in its new position. As I moved out I passed right in sight of a column of the Confederate forces, who evidently had come out of the hollow and were forming to again attack Vandever. They probably thought I was a portion of their force, for they made no demonstration towards me, and I passed right by them. As I passed out into the open I could see that General Asboth, who had been brought there by General Curtis, was forming to attack at the Elkhorn Tavern again; and I met General Curtis, who seemed astonished to find me with my force intact. He asked me where I was going. I told him that I was out of ammunition, and that I was bringing out my force to form it on the new line. Paying the command a high compliment, he immediately ordered me to fix bayonets and to charge on the enemy at the same time that Asboth with his reinforcement moved down the Fayetteville road towards the Elkhorn Tavern. I immediately did this, and passed right back over the field where I had been fighting, but found no enemy. They had evidently left my front at the same time I retired, and I returned and went into line on the right of Vandever's Brigade, probably 500 feet in the rear of the original line, and there we laid all night under arms.

Van Dorn's plan of attack was to throw the Arkansas forces under McCullough and McIntosh on Curtis's right, facing the Little Cross Hollow road, while at the same time General Price with his force moved around us by the Little Cross Timber road to our rear and attacked from the Cross Timbers.

When passing through Little Cross Timber Hollow Price struck the timber blockade, and, as he shows in his report, was held there for a long time before he could clear out the roads and get his forces and artillery through. This delayed his attack in the rear until nearly 10 o'clock in the morning. The two forces of McCullough and Price were separated by a high ridge by the name [Pg 23] of Pea Ridge, over which it was impracticable for them to connect, and, therefore, the two attacks were separate and not in concert.

General McCullough, in attacking from the west, struck General Jeff C. Davis's Division. Davis had a Division of troops that had been thoroughly drilled. He was a very competent officer and handled them with great skill, and the attack of McCullough and McIntosh, though desperate, was without avail, both rebel commanders being killed in the attack, which took all the fight out of the Arkansas troops and made their attacks towards evening of very little effect. Davis pursued them so energetically that after the death of their commanders they straggled off towards Arkansas and no more fighting occurred on that flank.

General Siegel's two Divisions had remained facing Sugar Creek. General Curtis had endeavored to bring them forward, but without avail. A Brigade of General Osterhaus's Division aided General Davis during the latter part of the day, but the Brigade from Asboth's Division did not get into line to help Carr until nearly dark, although General Curtis went in person for them. Colonel Carr's troops had been marching two nights before the battle, and on the night of the 7th he asked General Curtis to relieve them, so they could get some sleep. General Curtis promised they should be relieved by one of General Siegel's Divisions, but they held the line all that night right where they were formed, and when we looked for our relief the next morning we learned that General Siegel and his troops were nearly a mile in our rear, taking their breakfast.

The general plan of General Curtis's attack on the morning of the 8th was for a combined movement on Price's Army by both of General Siegel's Divisions, and General Davis, who had been brought over to our front, holding Carr's Division in reserve. We waited a long time for General Siegel to get into position; and in fact before he got into position Colonel Carr had been brought out from the reserve and placed on the right of Davis. The enemy opened out upon us, and my Brigade holding the right I commenced swinging my line in over the ground I had fought over the day before, and discovered that the enemy were withdrawing from us; were not standing and giving battle; and the fighting on the morning of the 8th was merely a fight of Price's rear-guard to enable him to withdraw by the Huntsville road, he having received orders that [Pg 24] morning from Van Dorn to do so, Van Dorn notifying Price that this was necessary, as the Arkansas troops, after the death of

McCullough and McIntosh, had most of them retreated to the south, leaving Price's Army the only force intact in our rear, so that he now had the difficult problem of getting away from us.

The fighting lasted but a short time, mostly with artillery, and occasioned very little loss for that day. We soon discovered the rebels fleeing over the hills and down the White River Road, and being nearest to that road I immediately started my Brigade after them. I had not proceeded far when I received an order from General Curtis to return and hold the battle-field. I was a good deal astonished at this, as I could see the enemy demoralized in my front, with their baggage-trains and their artillery, and I had no doubt, (as I knew the country, having had a detachment stationed at Blackburn's Mills, at the crossing of White River, supplying our Army with forage and grain before the battle,) that I could capture this portion of the army before it could make a crossing of White River.

When I arrived on the battle-field General Curtis told me that General Siegel and his Divisions had gone to the rear towards Cassville; in fact, I myself heard him give one of the Brigades that was passing an order to halt there, which they did not obey, but kept on. General Siegel wrote back advising Curtis to form his new line in the rear of Cross Timbers, as Van Dorn might return to the fight, but Curtis instructed Colonel Carr's Division to remain on the field and hold it, which it did. General Curtis afterwards made very severe complaints to General Halleck of the actions of General Siegel, and in answer General Halleck wrote as follows:

I was by no means surprised at General Siegel's conduct before the battle of Pea Ridge. It was plainly in keeping with what he did at Carthage and Wilson's Creek. After your expedition started I received documentary proof from Captains Sturgis, Schofield, and Totten, and a number of other officers, in regard to his conduct on those occasions, which destroyed all confidence in him. It was for that reason that I telegraphed to you so often not to let Siegel separate from you. I anticipated that he would try to play you a trick by being absent at the critical moment. I wished to forewarn you of the snare, but I could not then give you my reasons. I am glad you prevented his project and saved your army. I cannot describe to you how much uneasiness I felt for you. You saved your army and won a glorious victory by refusing to take his advice.

Captain Kinsman, of Company B, Fourth Iowa, who was holding Pea Ridge, and witnessed the battle from that point, and could [Pg 25] look down upon Carr's Division, described the battle in the rear as follows:

At 8:30 o'clock Colonel Dodge opened the ball, and the battle was soon raging all along the line with a fierceness and obstinacy which omened a terrific struggle. The weather was splendid, and the smoke instead of hanging murkily among the trees, rose rapidly and rolled away over the hills in dense sulphurous masses. The thunder of the artillery was terrific, and the shot and shell hissed and screamed through the air like flying devils, while the infantry of both armies, with their rifles, shot-guns, and muskets, kept a perfect hurricane of death howling through the woods. The rebels fought well, but generally fired too high, and their batteries, although getting our range accurately, missed the elevation much of the time. Their poor shooting was our salvation. Had they done as well as our men, with the tremendous odds against us, they must have annihilated us. The enemy were clear around our right flank, enveloping us, and it looked as though they would capture Dodge's Brigade, when Colonel Dodge took a battalion of Colonel Carr's regiment, the Third Illinois cavalry, and charged the forces that were turning our right flank like a whirlwind. Everything gave way before them. Every man in that battalion seemed to ride for his life, and they swept way around our front, routing and demoralizing that flank of the enemy, and effectually freeing our rear and flank. Price told some of our boys of the Fourth Iowa who were captured on the day of the fight and have since escaped, that we fought more like devils than human beings. The rebel colonels (several of them) inquired of our boys who those black-coated fellows were, and who led them. They said there must have been at least 3,000 of them. When the boys told them there were less than 600 of them, the Colonels said they needn't tell them any such stuff as that; that they knew it was a damned lie. But they sent their compliments to Colonel Dodge for the bravery of himself and his command, and well they might, for opposed to Colonel Dodge's Brigade of 1,050 men, and two guns of the First Iowa Battery, were six regiments of Confederate troops, a large force of Confederate Missouri State troops, and eighteen guns, and many of these Confederate troops were the men who did the hard fighting at the Wilson Creek battle. All day, from 8:30 in the morning till 5:30 at night, Dodge's Brigade held its ground, dealing death into the rebel ranks, and, when dark came, with ammunition expended, the Fourth Iowa walked away from the field in good order, with the sullen savage tread of men who might be driven by main strength, but could not be conquered. Although this was one of the first battles of the war, the Northern men showed their desperate fighting qualities; and on the second day the South met and faced great slaughter.

Fayel, the correspondent of the Missouri Democrat, gives this account of the part Colonel Eugene A. Carr's Fourth Iowa Division took in the battle at Elk Horn Tavern:

Having given an account of the battle fought by Brigadier-General Jeff C. Davis's Division, which occurred the same day, on our left, I will now attempt to give some details of the Elk Horn Battle—the latter having commenced early in the morning. First in order comes a description of the locality near Elk Horn Tavern.

The house is on the Fayetteville and Springfield road, about four miles north of Sugar Creek, between which two points our camp was pitched, on the elevated ridge constituting the northern bank of the creek. Leading north from the tavern, the road drops into the head of the long gorge running towards Keetsville seven miles, known as the "Cross Timbers."

Into the strong fastness north of the Tavern the enemy had obtained a lodgment from 10,000 to 15,000 strong in the rear of our wing, on the morning of the 7th. His strength consisted in part of the following rebel [Pg 26] Divisions, as was subsequently ascertained: Frost's, Slack's, Parson's, and Rains's; and the batteries of Ghebor, Clark (six pieces), E. McDonald (three pieces), and Wade (four pieces). There was present also one Regiment of Indians, the whole commanded by General Van Dorn in person, and General Price, who directs the Missouri forces.

Early in the morning, while General Curtis was in consultation with his officers regarding a change of front, consequent on the approach of the enemy on the west of us, news came that the enemy were in close vicinity to the Elk Horn Tavern. The General then immediately ordered Colonel Carr to proceed to effect a dislodgment of the enemy. The formidable numbers present at the time not being known, Colonel Carr directed Colonel Dodge, with the First Brigade of the Fourth Division, to take a position near the Elkhorn Tavern, Colonel Carr accompanying the expedition himself. The point indicated was about a mile and a half distant from our camp, the ground being level and gradually ascending, with open fields on either side of the road, interspersed with an occasional belt of timber.

Colonel Dodge having discovered the enemy in the timber to the right, opened the First Iowa Battery on them, causing considerable execution; two rebels on horseback were seen to fall, and the rest fled. The enemy having fled to the hollow, Colonel Dodge deployed his line, covering as much ground as possible, the Thirty-fifth Illinois being on his left. He sent forward a company of skirmishers from the Fourth Iowa, who soon became sharply engaged with the enemy and the latter opened on us a perfect tornado of round shot, shell, and grape. The Thirty-fifth Illinois became engaged, fighting with determined bravery, and about, this time Colonel Smith was wounded in the head by a shell, which took off a part of his scalp. He also received a bullet in his shoulder, and his horse was shot under him, all about the same time. Just before he was wounded, several ammunition-chests exploded, one after the other, wounding Captain Jones and Lieutenant Gamble, who were standing near Colonel Carr, the latter making a fortunate escape. The explosion of a caisson was terrific.

There was a short lull in the storm of leaden hail, during which time the enemy advanced up the hollow through the brush, along the main road, when Colonel Vandever, who had arrived, ordered forward the infantry. A desperate conflict with small arms ensued. Back rolled the tide of battle, the enemy being driven to the foot of the hill, when he reopened the batteries. Our men fought like heroes; many fell covered with wounds. The latter, when brought to the rear by their comrades, encouraged those who were still breasting the fierce cannonade, by hurrahing for the Union.

Colonel Vandever, in leading forward his brigade, had his horse hit twice, and Colonel Phelps, in the van of his own Regiment, had three horses shot under him. Major Geiger, of the same Regiment, and Captain Hayden, of the Dubuque Battery, had two horses shot under them. Major Coyle, of the Ninth Iowa, was wounded in the leg.

Colonel Dodge having discovered that the enemy were preparing for a general attack, changed his front to the right, covering his men with a log fence, thus compelling the enemy to cross an open field to reach him. Our line was formed and we opened fire with one section of a battery, the other pieces having left the field for want of ammunition. The enemy advanced on our right, left, and center, under cover of a destructive fire, poured in on our works under twelve pieces of artillery. The fighting now lasted over two hours, during which time we held our position; only one Brigade contending against at least six thousand rebel infantry and a heavy bombardment from their artillery, the latter playing upon us at short range. Our men fought like heroes without wincing under the galling fire belching forth from behind trees and rocks, and much of the time from a concealed foe. At one time we were reinforced by three rifled pieces from a German battery, which fired four rounds, and then was compelled to withdraw from the field, being flanked by a Regiment of the enemy.

[Pg 27] Colonel Dodge, in order to discover the position of the enemy on his right, directed his firing to cease, when a thousand rebel plush caps and black broad brims popped up into view from the bushes, and, forming, they advanced with great confidence to within one hundred feet of our line. Our men were then ordered to pour in a fire on the dastardly enemy, taking good aim. They were thrown into confusion by our murderous volley and fled.

Their places were filled by a fresh Regiment, and Colonel Dodge, finding that the enemy were outflanking him on the right and that his force was too weak to permit an extension of his line, sent for and soon received a reinforcement of five companies of the Eighth Indiana, which were posted on the right. The firing now became terrific. The enemy annoyed us severely by placing a battery on our left, which completely enfiladed our line. The Fourth Iowa now getting short of ammunition, and the Thirty-fifth Illinois having been forced to give way on the left, it was at this critical time that Lieutenant-Colonel Challenor was ordered to rally his men, who were hurled on the enemy, driving his left back a short distance. Having advanced too far, the Lieutenant-Colonel was surrounded and captured with forty of his men. Our ammunition, as before stated, having given out, we fell back to the open field, maintaining our line of battle in splendid order. The enemy rushed forward with their batteries and entire force. The Fourth Iowa halted, turned on them, and checked for a time their advance until the last round of ammunition was exhausted. General Curtis coming up about this stage of the action, was received with a round of cheers from our boys. The General learning that the ammunition had given out, ordered the Fourth Iowa to fix bayonets and charge on the enemy. The men did so briskly, across the field, but found no enemy.

On Colonel Vandever's front the enemy now commenced swarming up the road and along the gorge, and out of the brush in front of us. Our troops fought them bravely, the officers exposing their persons in leading in front of their men; but we were overwhelmed at this time by superior numbers. We retreated across the field, but rallied again along the fence behind our original position. Upon retiring as above mentioned, reinforcements were seen coming up under General Asboth. In a gallant attempt to resist the advancing column of the enemy, General Asboth received a severe wound in the arm. After the terrible conflict of the day our gallant troops bivouacked in front of the enemy, awaiting the reopening of the conflict in the morning.

Colonel Vandever fought Little's Division. Colonel Dodge's Brigade contended in the morning directly with Rain's and Clark's Divisions, both immediately under the direction of Sterling Price. The latter had his position for some time behind young Clarke's battery.

The enemy fired wagon-nuts, pieces of chain, marble, gravel, and all sorts of projectiles. The overcoat worn by Colonel Dodge was perfectly riddled by the jagged holes made by these unusual missiles.

Colonel Dodge, the day after the battle, received a letter from a widow lady in Illinois, stating that she had three sons in the field fighting for the Union; that her youngest son, who was in feeble health, was in his Brigade, and she asked it as a special favor to her in her loneliness to have him discharged. The young man whose mother had such solicitude in his behalf was named Preston Green, and was killed in the action of the 7th, near Elkhorn, while bravely performing his duty.

During the battle, Colonel Dodge's horse was shot under him. An enlisted man, detailed as clerk in the Adjutant's office, was acting as orderly for Colonel Dodge. When his horse fell, he ordered the orderly to dismount and give him his horse. The orderly said, "You will be killed if you get on another horse; this is the third you have lost." But the orderly dismounted and stood where the Colonel had stood when he asked for the horse, and at that moment was instantly killed by a shot from the enemy. After the battle, the Adjutant, Lieutenant Williamson, found in the orderly's [Pg 28] desk a note in which he said he was sure he would be killed in the battle, and in which, also, he left directions as to the disposal of his effects and whom to write to.

In General Price's command there was a Regiment or more of Indians commanded by Colonel Albert B. Pike. They crawled up through the thick timber and attacked my extreme left. I saw them and turned one of the guns of my battery on them, and they left. We saw no more of them, but they scalped and mutilated some of our dead. General Curtis entered a complaint to General Price, who answered that they were not of his command, and that they had scalped some of his dead, and he said he did not approve of their being upon the field. They evidently scalped many of the dead, no matter what side they belonged to.

The battle of Pea Ridge being one of the first of the war and one of unquestioned victory, had a great deal of attention called to it, and for months—in fact for years, and, I think even now—was considered to have been won by General Siegel. The proper credit was not given to General Curtis, while the history and records of the battle show that he was entitled to all of the credit, and fought the battle in opposition to Siegel's views. A statement of the losses shows what commands fought the battle. The total force engaged on our side, according to General Curtis's report, was 10,500 men, formed in four Divisions, Siegel's two Divisions being the largest, the Third and Fourth Divisions having less than 2,000 men each. The losses were:

First Division,* commanded by Osterhaus	144
Second Division,* commanded by Asboth	119
Third Division, commanded by Colonel Jeff C. Davis	329
Fourth Division, commanded by Colonel Carr	701

*Divisions were commanded by General Siegel.

Van Dorn's and Price's reports of the battle show how great their defeat was, and why it was, and while for some time General Curtis called anxiously on Halleck for more reinforcements, demanding that the column which was marching South in Kansas be sent to him, Van Dorn and Price, from the time they left the field, never stopped until they landed at Memphis, Tenn., their first movement being towards Pocahontas, with a view of attacking Pope in the rear, who was at New Madrid. Finding New Madrid captured, they turned their forces to Desarc, and were then transported by boats to Memphis. This relieved Missouri of any Confederate force in or near its border, and General Halleck immediately [Pg 29] gave General Curtis orders to move on the flank of Van Dorn and keep up with him, but through that swampy, hilly country it was impossible for him to meet Van Dorn, and Curtis with his Army finally landed at Helena, Ark., and most of it joined the Vicksburg siege.

Captain Phil Sheridan was the Quartermaster and Commissary of General Curtis's Army. He kept us in flour, meat, and meal, and sometimes had my whole regiment detailed in running and protecting mills, driving cattle, etc. He had great difficulty in obtaining details, as at that early day a good many commanders, and especially General Siegel and his officers, did not think it the duty of a soldier to be detailed on anything but a soldier's duty; so Sheridan naturally came to me, as he was my Quartermaster while I commanded the post at Rolla, and when with the marching column he camped and tented with me. Sheridan and Curtis had considerable difficulty, and Curtis relieved him and ordered him to report to General Halleck, at St. Louis. We who knew Sheridan's ability, and the necessities of our Army, did all we could to hold him with us. He left us just before the Battle of Pea Ridge, and our Army saw a great difference after he was gone. He used to say to me, "Dodge, if I could get into the line I believe I could do something;" and his ambition was to get as high a rank as I then had and as large a command—a Colonel commanding a Brigade. In his memoirs he pays the Fourth Iowa a great compliment, and says they will have a warm place in his heart during his life.

During the Battle of Pea Ridge Sheridan was at Springfield, Mo., preparing to turn over his property to the officer who was to relieve him, and he there showed his soldierly qualities. The dispatches from Curtis's army had to be relayed at Springfield. The first dispatches after the battle were sent all in praise of General Siegel, and by portions of his command, claiming he had won the battle. Sheridan, knowing this to be untrue, withheld the Siegel dispatches until the telegrams from General Curtis to General Halleck were received, and sent them forward first, notwithstanding the fact that he felt he had been unjustly treated by General Curtis.

This Army had no water or rail communication. It was 300 miles from its nearest supply-depot, and therefore it had to live off of a country that was sparsely settled by poor people; but Sheridan showed that dominant combination of enterprise and energy, [Pg 30] by running every mill and using every means of supply within fifty miles of us, that he developed so fully later in the war. He kept us and our stock fairly well supplied; as I remember, there were no complaints. When General Curtis concluded to relieve him, I went with others and endeavored to induce him to change his mind. I had had experience and knew what it was to have an Army well fed a long ways from its base, and I felt that if we lost Sheridan we would suffer, which later proved to be the case; but General Curtis did not listen to us. In fact, he was angry at our appeal, and his Adjutant, General McKinney, came to see us afterwards and urged us not to press the matter; if we did, he said, we might go to the rear with Sheridan.

At the Battle of Pea Ridge and during the campaign we were very destitute of all hospital appliances for the care of the wounded, and the ability and ingenuity of our medical staff in supplying our wants was inestimable. The day after the battle, when we had all our own wounded and so many of the enemy's with us, Mrs. Governor Phelps, the wife of Governor Phelps, of Missouri, who commanded the Twenty-fifth Missouri Infantry, arrived on the field with a general supply of sanitary goods, a part of which had been sent to my Regiment from Philadelphia by the father and mother of Captain Ford, who was then a Lieutenant in Company B, Fourth Iowa Infantry. These were a great relief, as fully one-third of my command were killed and wounded, and were suffering for want of this class of goods. Mrs. Phelps spent her time day and night on the field aiding the surgeons and succoring the wounded.

General Curtis endeavored to send all the wounded to the rear who could stand the trip. I was hauled 250 miles over a rough road in an ambulance, and if any of you have had the same experience you can judge what I suffered. Captain Burton, of my Regiment, who was severely wounded in the arm, sat on the front seat of that ambulance the whole distance, and never murmured, although he came near losing his arm from the exposure. It was during this ambulance trip, while lying on my back, that I received a telegraphic dispatch from General Halleck notifying me of my promotion for services in this battle. It was thought, and was also stated in the papers, that I could not live, and I told General Halleck afterwards that they expected to have the credit of making a Brigadier-General and at the same time to have a vacancy, [Pg 31] too, but that on the vacancy I fooled them, for the promotion insured my getting well.

This campaign demonstrated early in the war what could be accomplished by a small Army 300 miles away from any rail or water communication, in a rugged, mountainous, sparsely settled county, marching in winter, and virtually subsisting upon the country. Nothing escaped that Army that was eatable.

The Battle of Pea Ridge was fought by the two Divisions commanded by Carr and Davis, not exceeding 6,000 men, and it is a lesson in war that is very seldom appreciated: that no one can tell what the result of a battle may be, and that even where forces are very wide apart in numbers it is not always the larger force that wins. In this battle Van Dorn had put twice as many men into the fight as Curtis did, and still was defeated. His dividing his force and attacking our Army at two different points was fatal to his success, as General Curtis had the inside line and could move from one part of his command to another within an hour, while for Van Dorn to move from one portion of his Army to the other would have taken at least half a day, and therefore he was whipped in detail. If he had thrown his whole force upon Curtis's right flank at the point where McCullough fought and was overwhelmed by Davis's Division, there would have been great danger of our Army being defeated, or at least forced to the rear.

There was no strategy nor tactics in this battle; it was simply men standing up and giving and taking, and the one that stood the longest won the battle. The only strategy or tactics was the movement of Van Dorn attacking on the right flank and in the rear, and these moves were fatal to his success. Curtis's Army fought each man for himself. Every commander fought his own part of the battle to the best of his ability, and I think the feeling of all was that unless they won they would have to go to Richmond, as the enemy was in the rear, which fact made us desperate in meeting and defeating the continued attacks of the enemy. I sent for reinforcements once when the enemy was clear around my right flank and in my rear, and they sent me a part of the Eighth Indiana, two companies of the Third Illinois Cavalry, and a section of a battery. The battery fought ten minutes under a heavy fire. The four companies of the Eighth Indiana lined up alongside the Fourth Iowa, and stayed there fighting bravely until the end. The Third Illinois held my right flank. The officer who brought this [Pg 32] force to me was Lieutenant Shields, of my own Regiment, who was acting as aid on Colonel Carr's staff. As he rode up to me to report the Eighth Indiana he halted alongside of me, and at the same instant both of our horses fell dead without a struggle—something very unusual. I was quick, and jumped clear of my horse, but Shields's horse fell upon him. I walked away, not thinking of Shields; but he called back to me and said, "Colonel, you are not going to leave me this way are you?" and I returned and helped him from under his horse. An examination of the two horses made the next day, showed that they must have been killed by the same bullet, which passed through their necks at the same place, killing them instantly.

A log house was used by us early in the morning as a temporary hospital. When my skirmishers fell back this log house was left in the lines of the enemy, and Hospital Steward Baker, of the Fourth Iowa, was left in charge of the wounded there. When General Price came up he asked him who those black-coated devils were, and when Baker told him there were only six hundred he did not believe him. He said no six hundred men could stand such attacks, and paid the Brigade a very high compliment for their fighting, and told Baker to give them his compliments.

I never returned to this Army, but many of the troops who fought so gallantly fought afterwards in Corps and Armies that I was connected with. My own Regiment went into battle with 548 rank and file present. Company B was on detailed service holding Pea Ridge, and had no casualties in line of battle. My Regiment was greatly reduced from sickness and men on furlough, but the bravery and steadiness with which those with me fought was a surprise and a great satisfaction to me. One-third of them fell, and not a straggler left the field. I had drilled the Regiment to most all kinds of conditions—in the open, in the woods—and many complained, and thought I was too severe, as many Regiments at the posts where they were stationed only had the usual exercises; but after this, their first battle, they saw what drilling, maneuvers, and discipline meant, and they had nothing but praise for the severe drilling I had given them. They never fell under my command again, but on every field that they fought they won the praise of their commanders, and General Grant ordered that they should place on their banners, "First at Chickasaw Bayou."

[Pg 33] I have never thought that General Curtis has received the credit he was entitled to for this campaign and battle. With 12,000 men he traversed Missouri into Arkansas, living off the country, and showing good judgment in concentrating to meet Van Dorn and refusing to retreat when urged to do so at the conference at the log schoolhouse on the morning of the 7th. The night of the 7th I know some officers thought we ought to try to cut ourselves out to the East, Price being in our rear; but Curtis said he would fight where we were. He then had no knowledge of the condition of the enemy. On the morning of the 8th he brought General Siegel's two Divisions into the fight and concentrated on Price, whose fighting was simply to cover his retreat. General Curtis failed to reap the full benefit of the battle because Siegel went to Cassville, leaving only Davis's and Carr's Divisions on the field. We who took part in this campaign appreciate the difficulties and obstacles Curtis had to overcome, and how bravely and efficiently he commanded, and we honor him for it. So did General Halleck; but the Government, for some reason, failed to give him another command in the field, though they retained him in command of departments to the end of the war.

[Pg 34]

SYLVANUS DODGE

Father of Major-General G. M. Dodge.

[Pg 35]

Letter of General Grenville M. Dodge to his Father on the Battle of Pea Ridge

St. Louis, Mo., April 2, 1862.

DEAR FATHER:—I know there is no one who would like to have a word from me more than you. I write but little—am very weak from my wounds; do not sit up much; but I hope ere long to be all right again. Nothing now but the battle will interest you. It was a terrible three days to me; how I got through God only knows. I got off a sick bed to go to the fight, and I never got a wink of sleep for three days and three nights. The engagement was so long and with us so hot that it did not appear possible for us to hold our ground. We lacked sadly in numbers and artillery, but with good judgment and good grit we made it win. My officers were very brave. Little Captain Taylor would stand and clap his hands as the balls grew thick. Captain Burton was as cool as a cucumber, and liked to have bled to death; then the men, as they crawled back wounded, would cheer me; cheer for the Union; and always say, "Don't give up Colonel, hang to em;" and many who were too badly wounded to leave the field stuck to their places, sitting on the ground, loading and firing. I have heard of brave acts, but such determined pluck I never before dreamed of. My flag-bearer, after having been wounded so he could not hold up the colors, would not leave them. I had to peremptorily order him off. One time when the enemy charged through my lines the boys drove them back in confusion. Price fought bravely; his men deserved a better fate, but although two to one they could not gain much. Their artillery was served splendidly—they had great advantage over us in this. Mine run out of ammunition long before night and left me to the mercy of their grape and canister. Had I have had my full battery at night I could have whipped them badly. After the Fourth Iowa's ammunition gave out or before this all the other Regiments and Brigades had given way, leaving me without support, and when I found my ammunition gone I [Pg 36] never felt such a chilling in my life. It is terrible right in the midst of a hot contest to have your cartridges give out. We had fired forty-two rounds, and had but a few left. I saved them and ceased firing, falling back to my supports. The enemy charged me in full force. I halted and they came within fifty feet. We opened on them such a terrible fire they fled. General Curtis rode into the field then and asked me to charge. This would have blanched anybody but an Iowa soldier. No ammunition and to charge! We fixed bayo-

39

nets, and as I gave the order the boys cheered and cheered, swinging their hats in every direction. CHARGE! and such a yell as they crossed that field with, you never heard—it was unearthly and scared the rebels so bad they never stopped to fire at us or to let us reach them. As we marched back, now dark, nearly one-half the entire Army had got on the ground and the black-coats (Fourth Iowa) had got their fame up. The charge without ammunition took them all, and as we passed down the line the whole Army cheered us. General Curtis complimented us on the field, and what was left of the Fourth Iowa held their heads high that night, though a gloomy one for those who knew our situation. The next morning it fell to my lot to open the battle with my artillery again, and for one hour we poured it into them hot and heavy. We opened with thirty-two guns; they answered with as many, and such a roar you never heard. The enemy could not stand it and fled. Our whole army deployed in sight that morning and it was a grand sight with the artillery playing in open view. I had read of such things, but they were beyond my conception. This closed the battle and we breathed free. I escaped most miraculously. A shell burst right in front of me, and, tearing away my saddle holsters and taking off a large piece of my pants, never even scratched me. My clothes were riddled and I got a hit in the side that is serious, but did not think of it at the time.Yours, etc., G. M.

[Pg 37]

[Pg 38]

SIXTEENTH ARMY CORPS IN THE BATTLE OF ATLANTA

Painting by James E. Taylor for General William T. Sherman. This shows the time when Hardee's Corps, four Divisions, attacked the Sixteenth Army Corps in the rear of the Army of the Tennessee, and were defeated. General Dodge on horse in foreground ordering Colonel Mersey's brigade to charge one of the columns of the enemy in flank. Extreme right of picture, General Fuller's Division fighting General Walker's Division of the Confederate Army.

[Pg 39]

THE BATTLE OF ATLANTA

Fought July 22, 1864

A Paper Read Before New York Commandery M. O. L. L.

By Major-General Grenville M. Dodge

On the 17th day of July, 1864, General John B. Hood relieved General Joseph E. Johnston in command of the Confederate Army in front of Atlanta, and on the 20th Hood opened an attack upon Sherman's right, commanded by General Thomas. The attack was a failure, and resulted in a great defeat to Hood's Army and the disarrangement of all his plans.

On the evening of the 21st of July, General Sherman's Army had closed up to within two miles of Atlanta, and on that day Force's Brigade of Leggett's Division of Blair's Seventeenth Army Corps carried a prominent hill, known as Bald or Leggett's Hill, that gave us a clear view of Atlanta, and placed that city within range of our guns. It was a strategic point, and unless the swing of our left was stopped it would dangerously interfere with Hood's communications towards the south. Hood fully appreciated this, and determined upon his celebrated attack in the rear of General Sherman's Army.

On the 22d of July, the Army of the Tennessee was occupying the rebel intrenchments, its right resting very near the Howard House, north of the Augusta Railroad, thence to Leggett's Hill, which had been carried by Force's assault on the evening of the 21st. From this hill Giles A. Smith's Division of the Seventeenth Army Corps stretched out southward on a road that occupied this ridge, with a weak flank in air. To strengthen this flank, by order of General McPherson I sent on the evening of the 21st one Brigade of Fuller's Division, the other being left at Decatur to protect our [Pg 40] parked trains. Fuller camped his Brigade about half a mile in the rear of the extreme left and at right angles to Blair's lines and commanding the open ground and valley of the forks of Sugar Creek, a position that proved very strong in the battle. Fuller did not go into line; simply bivouacked ready to respond to any call.

On the morning of the 22d of July, General McPherson called at my headquarters and gave me verbal orders in relation to the movement of the Second (Sweeney's) Division of my command, the Sixteenth Corps, which had been crowded out of the line by the contraction of our lines as we neared Atlanta, and told me that I was to take position on the left of the line that Blair had been instructed to occupy and intrench that morning, and cautioned me about protecting my flank very strongly. McPherson evidently thought that there would be trouble on that flank, for he rode out to examine it himself.

I moved Sweeney in the rear of our Army, on the road leading from the Augusta Railway down the east branch of Sugar Creek to near where it forks; then, turning west, the road crosses the west branch of Sugar Creek just back of where Fuller was camped, and passed up through a strip of woods and through Blair's lines near where his left was refused. Up this road Sweeney marched until he reached Fuller, when he halted, waiting until the line I had selected on Blair's proposed new left could be intrenched, so that at mid-day, July 22d, the position of the Army of the Tennessee was as follows: One Division of the Fifteenth across and north of the Augusta Railway facing Atlanta; the balance of the Fifteenth and all of the Seventeenth Corps behind intrenchments running south of the railway along a gentle ridge with a gentle slope and clear valley facing Atlanta in front, and another clear valley in the rear. The Sixteenth Corps was resting on the road described, entirely in the rear of the Seventeenth and Fifteenth Corps, and facing from Atlanta. To the left and left-rear the country was heavily wooded. The enemy, therefore, was enabled, under cover of the forest, to approach close to the rear of our lines.

On the night of July 21st Hood had transferred Hardee's Corps and two Divisions of Wheeler's Cavalry to our rear, going around our left flank, Wheeler attacking Sprague's Brigade of the Sixteenth Army Corps at Decatur, where our trains were parked. At daylight, Stewart's and Cheatham's Corps and the Georgia Militia were withdrawn closer to Atlanta, and placed in a position [Pg 41] to attack simultaneously with Hardee, the plan thus involving the destroying of the Army of the Tennessee by attacking it in rear and front and the capturing of all its trains corraled at Decatur. Hardee's was the largest Corps in Hood's Army, and according to Hood there were thus to move upon the Army of the Tennessee about 40,000 troops.

Hood's order of attack was for Hardee to form entirely in the rear of the Army of the Tennessee, but Hardee claims that he met Hood on the night of the 21st; that he was so late in moving his Corps that they changed the plan of attack so that his left was to strike the Seventeenth Corps. He was to swing his right until he enveloped and attacked the rear of the Seventeenth and Fifteenth Corps.

Hood stood in one of the batteries of Atlanta, where he could see Blair's left and the front line of the Fifteenth and Seventeenth Corps. He says he was astonished to see the attack come on Blair's left instead of his rear, and charges his defeat to that fact; but Hardee, when he swung his right and came out in the open, found the Sixteenth Corps in line in the rear of our Army, and he was as much surprised to find us there as our Army was at the sudden attack in our rear. The driving back by the Sixteenth Corps of Hardee's Corps made the latter drift to the left and against Blair,—not only to Blair's left, but into his rear,—so that what Hood declares was the cause of his failure was not Hardee's fault, as his attacks on the Sixteenth Corps were evidently determined and fierce enough to relieve him from all blame in that matter.

Historians and others who have written of the Battle of Atlanta have been misled by being governed in their data by the first dispatches of General Sherman, who was evidently misinformed, as he afterwards corrected his dispatches. He stated in the first dispatch that the attack was at 11 a. m., and on Blair's Corps, and also that General McPherson was killed about 11 a. m. The fact is, Blair was not attacked until half an hour after the attack upon the Sixteenth Corps, and McPherson fell at about 2 p. m. General Sherman was at the Howard House, which was miles away from the scene of Hardee's attack in the rear, and evidently did not at first comprehend the terrific fighting that was in progress, and the serious results that would have been effected had the attack succeeded.

The battle began within fifteen or twenty minutes of 12 o'clock (noon) and lasted until midnight, and covered the ground from [Pg 42] the Howard House along the entire front of the Fifteenth (Logan's) Corps, the Seventeenth (Blair's) on the front of the Sixteenth (which was formed in the rear of the Army), and on to Decatur, where Sprague's Brigade of the Sixteenth Army Corps met and defeated Wheeler's Cavalry—a distance of about seven miles.

The Army of the Tennessee had present on that day at Atlanta and Decatur about 26,000 men; there were 10,000 in the Fifteenth Army Corps, 9,000 in the Sixteenth Corps, and 7,000 in the Seventeenth. About 21,000 of these were in line of battle. Three Brigades of the Sixteenth Corps were absent, the Sixteenth Corps having 5,000 men in a single line which received the attack of the four Divisions of Hardee's Corps, Hardee's left, Cleburn's Division lapping the extreme left of Blair and joining Cheatham's Corps which attacked Blair from the Atlanta front; and, according to Hood, they were joined by the Georgia Militia under General Smith. Extending down the line in front of the Armies of the Ohio and the Cumberland, Stewart's Corps occupied the works and held the lines in front of the Army of the Cumberland. The Sixteenth Army Corps fought in the open ground; the Fifteenth and Seventeenth behind intrenchments.

Where I stood just at the rear of the Sixteenth Army Corps, I could see the entire line of that corps, and could look up and see the enemy's entire front as they emerged from the woods, and I quickly saw that both of my flanks were overlapped by the enemy. Knowing General McPherson was some two miles away, I sent a staff officer to General Giles A. Smith, requesting him to refuse his left and protect the gap between the Seventeenth Corps and my right, which he sent word he would do. Later, as the battle progressed, and I saw no movement on the part of General Smith, I sent another officer to inform him that the enemy were passing my right flank, which was nearly opposite his center, and requested him to refuse his left immediately, or he would be cut off. This officer (Lieutenant D. Sheffly, who belonged to the Signal Corps, and acted as my aide only for the time being) found, on reaching Smith, that he was just becoming engaged; that he had received orders to hold his line, with a promise that other troops would be thrown into the gap.

My second messenger, Lieutenant Sheffly, returning over the road upon which McPherson was a few minutes later shot dead, [Pg 43] met the General on the road with a very few attendants, and turned to warn him of his dangerous position, assuring him that the enemy held the woods and were advancing. The General paying no heed to the warning and moving on, my aide turned and followed him. They had proceeded but a short distance into the woods when a sharp command, "Halt," was heard from the skirmish-line of the rebels. Without heeding the command, General McPherson and his party wheeled their horses, and at that moment a heavy volley was poured in, killing McPherson and so frightening the horses that they became unmanageable and plunged into the underbrush in different directions. My aide became separated from the General and the rest of the party, and was knocked from his horse by coming in contact with a tree, and lay for some time in an unconscious condition on the ground. As soon as he was sufficiently recovered he returned on foot to me, having lost his horse and equipments. Of General McPherson he saw nothing after his fall. His watch, crushed by contact with the tree, was stopped at two minutes past 2 o'clock, which fixed the time of General McPherson's death.

General McPherson could not have left his point of observation more than a few minutes when I detected the enemy's advance in the woods some distance to my right, and between that flank and General Blair's rear. Fuller quickly changed front with a portion of his brigade to confront them, and pushing promptly to the attack captured their skirmish-line and drove back their main force. Upon the persons of some of these prisoners we found McPherson's papers, field-glass, etc., which conveyed to me the first knowledge I had of his death; or, rather, as I then supposed, of his capture by the enemy; and seeing that the papers were important I sent them by my Chief of Staff with all haste to General Sherman.

General McPherson, it seems, had just witnessed the decisive grapple of the Sixteenth Corps with the charging columns of the enemy, and, as probably conveying his own reflections at that moment, I quote the language of General Strong, the only staff officer present with him at that critical time:

The General and myself, accompanied only by our orderlies, rode on and took positions on the right of Dodge's line, and witnessed the desperate assaults of Hood's army.

The Divisions of Generals Fuller and Sweeney were formed in a single line of battle in the open fields, without cover of any kind (Fuller's Division on the right,) and were warmly engaged. The enemy, massed in columns three or four lines deep, moved out of the dense timber several hundred yards from General Dodge's position, and after gaining fairly the open fields, halted and opened a rapid fire upon the Sixteenth Corps. They, however, [Pg 44] seemed surprised to find our infantry in line of battle, prepared for attack, and after facing for a few minutes the destructive fire from the Divisions of Generals Fuller and Sweeney, fell back in disorder to the cover of the woods. Here, however, their lines were quickly reformed, and they again advanced, evidently determined to carry the position.

The scene at this time was grand and impressive. It seemed to us that every mounted officer of the attacking column was riding at the front of, or on the right or left of, the first line of battle. The regimental colors waved and fluttered in advance of the lines, and not a shot was fired by the rebel infantry, although the movement was covered by a heavy and well-directed fire from artillery, which was posted in the woods and on higher ground, and which enabled the guns to bear upon our troops with solid shot and shell, firing over the attacking column.

It seemed impossible, however, for the enemy to face the sweeping, deadly fire from Fuller's and Sweeney's Divisions, and the guns of the Fourteenth Ohio and Welker's Batteries of the Sixteenth Corps fairly mowed great swaths in the advancing columns. They showed great steadiness, and closed up the gaps and preserved their alignments; but the iron and leaden hail which was poured upon them was too much for flesh and blood to stand, and, before reaching the center of the open field, the columns were broken up and thrown into great confusion. Taking advantage of this, General Dodge, with portions of General Fuller's and General Sweeney's Divisions, with bayonets fixed, charged the enemy and drove them back to the woods, taking many prisoners.

General McPherson's admiration for the steadiness and determined bravery of the Sixteenth Corps was unbounded. General Dodge held the key to the position.

Had the Sixteenth Corps given way the rebel army would have been in the rear of the Seventeenth and Fifteenth Corps, and would have swept like an avalanche over our supply trains, and the position of the Army of the Tennessee would have been very critical, although, without doubt, the result of the battle would have been in our favor, because the Armies of the Cumberland and the Ohio were close at hand, and the enemy would have been checked and routed further on.

General Blair, in his official report of the battle, says:

I witnessed the first furious assault upon the Sixteenth Army Corps, and its prompt and gallant repulse. It was a fortunate circumstance for that whole army that the Sixteenth Army Corps occupied the position I have attempted to describe, at the moment of the attack; and although it does not become me to comment upon the brave conduct of the officers and men of that Corps, still I can not refrain from expressing my admiration for the manner in which the Sixteenth Corps met and repulsed the repeated and persistent attacks of the enemy.

The Sixteenth Corps has a record in that battle which we seldom see in the annals of war. It met the shock of battle and fired the last shot late that night, as the enemy stubbornly yielded its grasp on Bald Hill. It fought on four parts of the field, and everywhere with equal success. It lost no gun that it took into the engagement, and its losses were almost entirely in killed and wounded—the missing having been captured at Decatur through getting mired in a swamp.

At no time during the Atlanta campaign was there present in the Sixteenth Corps more than two small Divisions of three Brigades [Pg 45] each, and at this time these two Divisions were widely scattered; on the Atlanta field only ten Regiments and two Batteries were present, three entire Brigades being absent from the Corps. It was called upon to meet the assault of at least three Divisions or nine Brigades, or at the least forty-nine Regiments, all full to the utmost that a desperate emergency could swell them, impelled by the motive of the preconcerted surprise, and orders from their commander at all hazards to sweep over any and all obstructions; while, on the other hand, the force attacked and surprised was fighting without orders, guided only by the exigency of the moment. Their captures represented forty-nine different Regiments of the enemy. How many more Regiments were included in those nine Brigades I have never been able to learn. The fact that this small force, technically, if not actually, in march, in a perfectly open field, with this enormously superior force leaping upon them from the cover of dense woods, was able to hold its ground and drive its assailants, pell-mell, back to the cover of the woods again, proves that when a great battle is in progress, or a great emergency occurs, no officer can tell what the result may be when he throws in his forces, be they 5,000 or 20,000 men; and it seems to me to be impossible to draw the line that gives the right to a subordinate officer to use his own judgment in engaging an enemy when a great battle is within his hearing.

Suppose the Sixteenth Corps, with less than 5,000 men, seeing at least three times their number in their front, should have retreated, instead of standing and fighting as it did: What would have been the result? I say that in all my experience in life, until the two forces struck and the Sixteenth Corps stood firm, I never passed more anxious moments.

Sprague's Brigade, of the same corps, was engaged at the same time within hearing, but on a different field, — at Decatur, — fighting and stubbornly holding that place, knowing that if he failed the trains massed there and *en route* from Roswell would be captured. His fight was a gallant and sometimes seemingly almost hopeless one — giving ground inch by inch, until, finally, he obtained a position that he could not be driven from, and one that protected the entire trains of the Army.

As Hardee's attack fell upon the Sixteenth Army Corps, his left Division (Cleburn's) lapped over and beyond Blair's left, and swung around his left front; they poured down through the gap [Pg 46] between the left of the Seventeenth and the right of the Sixteenth Corps, taking Blair in front, flank, and rear. Cheatham's Corps moved out of Atlanta and attacked in Blair's front. General Giles A. Smith commanded Blair's left Division, his right connecting with Leggett at Bald Hill, where Leggett's Division held the line until they connected with the Fifteenth Corps, and along this front the battle raged with great fury.

As Cleburn advanced along the open space between the Sixteenth and Seventeenth Corps they cut off from Blair's left and captured a portion of two Regiments of his command, and forced the Seventeenth Corps to form new lines, utilizing the old intrenchments thrown up by the enemy, fighting first on one side and then on the other, as the attack would come from Hardee in the rear or Cheatham in the front, until about 3:30 p. m., when, evidently after a lull, an extraordinary effort was made by the rebels to wipe out Giles A. Smith's Division and capture Leggett's Hill, the enemy approaching under cover of the woods until they were within fifty yards of Smith's temporary position, when they pressed forward until the fight became a hand-to-hand conflict across the trenches occupied by Smith, the troops using bayonet freely and the officers their swords. This attack failed; it was no doubt timed to occur at the same time that Cheatham's Corps attacked from the Atlanta front, which Leggett met. The brunt of Cheatham's attack was against Leggett's Hill, the key to the position of that portion of the Army of the Tennessee. General Giles A. Smith's Division had to give up the works they occupied and fall into line at right angles with Leggett's Division, Leggett's Hill being the apex of the formation; and around this position for three-quarters of an hour more desperate fighting was done that I can describe. Up to midnight the enemy occupied one side of the works while we occupied the other, neither side giving way until Hood saw that the whole attack was a failure, when those who were on the outside of the works finally surrendered to us. Their attack at this angle was a determined and resolute one, advancing up to our breastworks on the crest of the hill, planting their flag side by side with ours, and fighting hand to hand until it grew so dark that nothing could be seen but the flash of guns from the opposite sides of the works. The ground covered by these attacks was literally strewn with the dead of both sides. The loss of Blair's Corps was 1,801 killed, wounded, and missing. Blair's left struck in the rear flank, [Pg 47] and the front gave way slowly, gradually, fighting for every inch of ground, until their left was opposite the right flank of the Sixteenth Corps; then they halted, and held the enemy, refusing to give another inch.

It would be difficult in all the annals of war to find a parallel to the fighting of the Seventeenth Corps; first from one side of its works and then from the other, one incident of which was that of Colonel Belknap, of the Union side, who, reaching over the works, seized the Colonel of the Forty-fifth Alabama, and, drawing him over the breastworks, made him a prisoner of war.

About 4 p. m. Cheatham's Corps was ordered by Hood to again attack; they directed their assault this time to the front of the Fifteenth Corps, using the Decatur wagon-road and railway as a guide, and came forward in solid masses, meeting no success until they slipped through to the rear of the Fifteenth Corps by a deep cut used by the railway passing through our intrenchments.

As soon as they reached our rear, Lightburn's Division of the Fifteenth Corps became partially panic-stricken, and fell back, giving up the intrenchments for the whole front of this Division, the enemy capturing the celebrated Degress Battery of 20-pounders and two guns in advance of our lines. The officers of Lightburn's Division rallied it in the line of intrenchments, just in the rear of the position they had in the morning.

General Logan was then in command of the Army of the Tennessee. He rode over to my position, and I sent Mersey's Brigade of the Second Division, under the guidance of Major Edward Jonas, my Aide-de-camp, to the aid of the Fifteenth Corps. Of the performance of that Brigade on that occasion, I quote the words of that staff officer, Major Jonas:

I conducted Mersey's Brigade to the point where needed; arrived at the railroad, he at once deployed and charged, all men of the Fifteenth Corps at hand joining with him. Mersey's Brigade recaptured the works and the guns. Old Colonel Mersey was slightly wounded, and his celebrated horse, "Billy," killed. By your direction I said to General Morgan L. Smith (temporarily in command of the Fifteenth Corps): "General Dodge requests that you return this Brigade at the earliest practicable moment, as there is every indication of renewed assault on our own line," and, after saying that your request would be respected, General Smith added: "Tell General Dodge that his Brigade (Mersey's) has done magnificently, and that it shall have full credit in my report."

Afterwards one of Mersey's officers—Captain Boyd, I think—in trying his skill as an artillerist, cracked one of the recaptured guns. At the same moment of Mersey's attack in front, General [Pg 48] Wood's Division of the Fifteenth Army Corps, under the eye of General Sherman, attacked the Confederates occupying our intrenchments in flank, and Williamson's Brigade joined Mersey's in recapturing our line and the batteries—the Fourth Iowa Infantry taking a conspicuous part.

Colonel Mersey and many of his men whom he so gallantly led had served their time before this battle occurred, and were awaiting transportation home. Eloquent words have been written and spoken all over the land in behalf of the honor and the bravery of the soldier; but where is the word spoken or written that can say more for the soldier than the action of these men on that field? They were out of service; they had written that they were coming home, and their eyes and hearts were toward the North. Many an anxious eye was looking for the boy who voluntarily laid down his life that day, and many a devoted father, mother or sister has had untold trouble to obtain recognition in the War Department because the soldier's time had expired. He was mustered out; waiting to go home; and was not known on the records; but on that day he fought on three different parts of the field, without a thought except for his cause and his country.

The continuous attacks of Cheatham made no other impression on the line. Our men were behind the intrenchments and the slaughter of the enemy was something fearful. General J. C. Brown, who commanded the Confederate Division that broke through our line, told me that after breaking through it was impossible to force his men forward; the fire on their flanks and front was so terrific that when driven out of the works one-half of his command was killed, wounded, or missing. The Confederate records sustain this, and it is a wonder that they could force their line so often up to within 100 to 300 feet of us, where our fire would drive them back in spite of the efforts of their officers, a great many of whom fell in these attacks.

I could see the terrific fighting at Leggett's Hill, but of that along the line of the Fifteenth Corps I can only speak from the records and as told me by General John C. Brown, of the Confederate Army. The stubbornness and coolness with which they contested every inch of the ground won his admiration, and the manner and method with which the line was retaken must have been seen to be appreciated.

[Pg 49] When darkness fell upon us the enemy had retired, except around the angle in the Seventeenth Corps, known as Leggett's or

Bald Hill. Here there was a continuous fire, desultory and at close quarters, the enemy in places occupying ground close up to our intrenchments. To relieve these men of the Seventeenth Army Corps holding this angle, who were worn out, at the request of General Blair I sent two Regiments of Mersey's Brigade. They crawled in on their hands and knees, and swept the enemy from that front.

The whole of Hood's Army, except Stewart's Corps, was thrown into our rear, upon the flank and the front of the Army of the Tennessee, and after fighting from mid-day until dark were repulsed and driven back. That Army held or commanded the entire battlefield, demonstrating the fact that the Army of the Tennessee alone was able and competent to meet and defeat Hood's entire Army. The battle fell almost entirely upon the Sixteenth and Seventeenth Corps and two Divisions of the Fifteenth Corps, three Brigades of the Sixteenth being absent. The attack of the enemy was made along this line some seven times, and they were seven times repulsed.

We captured eighteen stands of colors, 5,000 stands of arms, and 2,017 prisoners. We lost in killed and wounded 3,521 men and ten pieces of artillery, and over 1,800 men, mostly from Blair's Corps, were taken prisoners. The enemy's dead reported as buried in front of the different Corps was over 2,000, and the enemy's total loss in killed, wounded and prisoners was 8,000.

The criticism has often been made of this battle that with two Armies idle that day, one the Army of the Ohio (two-thirds as large as the Army of the Tennessee) and the other the Army of the Cumberland (the largest of all Sherman's Armies), why we did not enter Atlanta. General Sherman urged Thomas to make the attack; Thomas's answer was that the enemy were in full force behind his intrenchments. The fact was that Stewart's Corps was guarding that front, but General Schofield urged Sherman to allow him to throw his Army upon Cheatham's flank, in an endeavor to roll up the Confederate line and so interpose between Atlanta and Cheatham's Corps, which was so persistently attacking the Fifteenth and Seventeenth Corps from the Atlanta front. Sherman, whose anxiety had been very great, seeing how successfully we were meeting the attack, his face relaxing into a pleasant smile, said to [Pg 50] Schofield, "Let the Army of the Tennessee fight it out this time." This flank attack of Schofield on Cheatham would have no doubt cleared our front facing the Atlanta intrenchments, but Stewart was ready with his three Divisions and the Militia to hold them.

General Sherman, in speaking of this battle, always regretted that he did not allow Schofield to attack as he suggested, and also force the fighting on Thomas's front; but no doubt the loss of McPherson really took his attention from everything except the Army of the Tennessee.

At about 10 o'clock on the night of the 22d, the three Corps commanders of the Army of the Tennessee (one of them in command of the Army) met in the rear of the Fifteenth Corps, on the line of the Decatur road, under an oak tree, and there discussed the results of the day. Blair's men were at the time in the trenches; in some places the enemy held one side and they the other. The men of the Fifteenth Corps were still in their own line, but tired and hungry, and those of the Sixteenth were, after their hard day's fight, busy throwing up intrenchments on the field they had held and won. It was thought that the Army of the Cumberland and the Army of the Ohio, which had not been engaged that day, should send a force to relieve Blair, and Dodge, being the junior Corps commander, was dispatched by General Logan, at the requests of Generals Logan and Blair, to see General Sherman. My impression is that I met him in a tent; I have heard it said that he had his headquarters in a house. When I met him he seemed rather surprised to see me, but greeted me cordially, and spoke of the loss of McPherson. I stated to him my errand. He turned upon me and said, "Dodge, you whipped them today, didn't you?" I said, "Yes, sir." Then he said: "Can't you do it again tomorrow?" and I said, "Yes, sir"; bade him good-night, and went back to my command, determined never to go upon another such errand. As he explained it afterward, he wanted it said that the little Army of the Tennessee had fought the great battle that day, needing no help, no aid, and that it could be said that all alone it had whipped the whole of Hood's Army. Therefore, he let us hold our position and our line, knowing that Hood would not dare attack us after the "thrashing" he had already received. When we consider that in this, the greatest battle of the campaign, the little Army of the Tennessee met the entire rebel Army, secretly thrust to its rear, on its flank, and upon its advance center, with its idolized commander

[Pg 51] killed in the first shock of battle, and at nightfall found the enemy's dead and wounded on its front, we see that no disaster — no temporary rebuff — could discourage this Army. Every man was at his post; every man doing a hero's duty. They proved they might be wiped out but never made to run. They were invincible.

Companions, regarding so great a battle, against such odds, with such loss, the question has often been asked me — and I know it has come to the mind of all of us — why it was that this battle was never put forth ahead of many others inferior to it, but better known to the world and causing much greater comment?

The answer comes to all of us. It is apparent to us today, as it was that night. We had lost our best friend, — that superb soldier, our commander, General McPherson; his death counted so much more to us than victory that we spoke of our battle, our great success, with our loss uppermost in our minds.

[Pg 52]

MONUMENT ERECTED ON THE BATTLE-FIELD OF ATLAN-TA

This monument was erected by the Society of the Army of the Tennessee on the spot where Major-General James B. McPherson was killed, July 22, 1864.

LETTER TO GENERAL RAUM

Correcting Some Statements
In
General Green B. Raum's
Description of the Battle of Atlanta
Published
In the National Tribune, Washington, D. C.
September 25, 1902

My Dear General:

Referring to my conversation with you in Washington, I will endeavor to aid you in getting at the actual facts connected with the Battle of Atlanta, as it has never yet been properly written up.

I delivered an address on September 25th, 1889, to the Army of the Tennessee on that battle, copy of which I am sending to you, and from which I think you can get a good deal of information.

I first want to call your attention to the fact that the battle commenced about fifteen minutes after 12 o'clock, and that the Sixteenth Army Corps fought a long time before the Seventeenth Corps was attacked. You can verify this statement by reading General Strong's account of the battle, which is given in our Army of the Tennessee records, volume 11 to 13, page 242.

It was just 12 o'clock exactly when I reached Fuller's headquarters. Having gone to the front to select my position, Fuller asked me to stop and take luncheon, and I got down from my horse and went into his tent. I had sat down at the table when I heard skirmish firing in the rear. Fuller said it was a lot of the boys out there killing hogs. The stillness had been oppressive as we went clear to the left and front of Blair's line to select my new position. We inquired from the pickets and found that nobody had seen anything of the enemy. It made an impression on us all; so the moment I heard this firing I jumped up, as if by instinct, and told [Pg 54] Fuller to get into line, and sent a staff officer towards Sweeney; but before he hardly got out of the tent Sweeney was in line and fighting, so you can see how sudden the attack was.

In volume 11 to 13 of the Army of the Tennessee records, page 243, Strong, in his address on the Battle of Atlanta, has this to say fixing the time of the commencement of the battle, speaking of the time when an officer was sent with an order to me from McPherson:

The officer had hardly disappeared from sight, when a shot was heard to the left and rear of us, then another, followed quickly by a rattling volley of small arms, and at almost the same instant a shell came crashing through the tree-tops near us, followed by a rapid and incessant firing from Dodge's Corps. At the first shots every officer sprang to his feet and called for his horse. The time, I should think, was ten or fifteen minutes past 12 o'clock.

Then after speaking of the fighting of this Division, comes this, on page 243:

After the *two* attempts to break the Sixteenth Corps had failed, General McPherson sent me to General Blair to ascertain the condition of affairs along his line, and instructed me to say to General Giles A. Smith to hold his position; that he would order up troops to occupy the gap between the Seventeenth and Sixteenth Corps; and also saying as I left him that he would remain with his orderly where he then was (a commanding position on Dodge's right) until I returned. I rode rapidly through the woods towards the Seventeenth Corps and found General Blair with General Giles A. Smith near the extreme left of the Fourth Division (Hall's Brigade).

This conclusively shows that Blair was not attacked until after two attacks had been made upon me, although Hall's report gives the attack upon Blair as at 12 o'clock, that time being before the Sixteenth Corps was attacked. Fuller gives the time of attack upon him as 12:30. By reading all of page 243 you will get a full and clear idea of time and everything. The time was also taken by my staff and record made of it, and that agrees with Strong. This only shows how far apart officers can get as to time in a great battle, and on many things, unless correct data is made of record on the spot.

On page 484, of volume 14 to 16 of Society of the Army of the Tennessee records, General Leggett says:

Both divisions of the Sixteenth Army Corps immediately became hotly engaged.... Just at this time I espied General McPherson upon the high ground in the immediate rear of General Fuller's command, and sent Captain John B. Raymond of my staff to inquire of General McPherson the expediency of having General Giles A. Smith and myself change our line so as to face south, and at the same time I sent Captain George W. Porter to ascertain whether or not the left of General Smith and the right of General Fuller were sufficiently near together to antagonize any force seeking [Pg 55] entrance there.... The enemy in front of the Sixteenth Corps rallied in the woods (this is after the first attack) and renewed their attack with increased vigor and bitterness.... The conflict continued for some time, with no appearance on either side of any disposition to yield the ground, when the enemy gave way, and fell back in confusion, followed by the Sixteenth Corps.... The second assault (upon the Sixteenth Corps) was simultaneous with the attack upon General Giles A. Smith's Division, which was the left of the Seventeenth Corps.

You will note from my address that the moment I was attacked I sent an aide, and afterwards a signal officer named Sheffly (I think), who was detailed with me that day, or happened to be with me. These officers had gone to General Giles A. Smith, who commanded Blair's left, Fourth Division, Seventeenth Corps, to get him to refuse his left and join my right. I think the first officer I sent was Captain Jonas of my staff, who returned immediately to me, and General Giles A. Smith sent me word that he would refuse. That was a long time before Cleburn's Division got between us; but, as my paper and your article show, McPherson had sent word to Giles A. Smith without knowing the condition in his front, to hold his position, stating that he would send reinforcements to fill the gap between Fuller and himself. Of course, had McPherson been there earlier and seen what I saw, he would have had Smith's left join my right immediately, which would have put Cleburn in front of us instead of between us. That is one of the things that occur in battle that the person on the ground knows better than the one distant. It was on the third attack on my line that the enemy struck Blair, as Strong did not go to Blair until after the repulse of the second attack. Cleburn's force got right in behind Blair's left and picked up that portion of his line that was refused, and swept back his force so that Blair's left, even before Waglin of the Fifteenth Corps got there, was pretty nearly an extension of but a quarter of a mile away from Fuller's right, and after I got through fighting I had to withdraw my entire right quite a distance to connect with Waglin and Blair, as Cleburn's force had pressed clear beyond me and before he was halted was way in the rear of my right.

After the second attack, Cleburn, as he pressed through the gap between Fuller and Smith, forced Fuller to change front and use part of his force to protect his flank, and the Sixty-fourth Illinois in this movement captured the skirmish-line that killed McPherson, taking from them his field-glass, orders, and other papers that they had taken from McPherson's body; and later in the [Pg 56] day I sent these to General Sherman. See report Sixty-fourth Illinois, volume 38, part 3, War Records, page 494. Fuller's maps, page 480, volume 38, part 3, War Records, show where Fuller fought, and where we had to intrench.

Where I stood in my line I could see the entire Confederate force, and all of my own, something that very seldom occurs, and, of course, the scene, as Blair states, was a magnificent one. I saw Fuller do a most gallant act. I sent an aide to him with instructions to charge, but before he got there Walker's division broke the center of Fuller's Brigade, his own regiment, the Twenty-seventh Ohio, falling back. I saw Fuller get down off his horse, grab the colors of the Twenty-seventh, rush to the front with them in his hands, and call upon his regiment to come to the colors; and they rallied and saved his front. It was but a moment later that I saw Walker, who commanded the division that was attacking Fuller, fall from his horse, and the division broke and went into the woods. The action of Fuller was very gallant, and has been painted, and I have a copy of the painting in my room.

Blair in his report has this to say of the fighting, which shows that he watched us a long time before he was attacked; and if you will read his report carefully, you will see that it bears out my statements in full:

I started to go back to my command and witnessed the fearful assault made on the Sixteenth Army Corps, and its prompt and gallant repulse by that command. It was a most fortunate circumstance for the whole army that the Sixteenth Army Corps occupied the position I have attempted to describe at the moment of attack, and although it does not belong to me to report upon the bearing and conduct of the officers and men of that Corps, still I cannot withhold my expression of admiration for the manner in which this command met and repulsed the repeated and persistent attacks of the enemy. The attack upon our flank was made by the whole of Hardee's Corps.

I speak in my address of Mercer's Brigade fighting on three parts of the field. Mercer, after helping to retake the Decatur-road line, camped right in the rear of the Fifteenth Corps, and did not come back to me. When Logan, Blair and myself met that evening, Blair asked Logan for some help to go up to relieve troops at Bald Hill. Logan, seeing Mercer's Brigade there, ordered me to send it up. They went up there and crawled in and relieved the men on Bald Hill. This was very late in the night, and even then fresh men coming in drove out or captured what men there were still lying on the enemy's side of the intrenchments. Mercer never made a report of this battle. You will see by my paper that he [Pg 57] was virtually out of the service, awaiting transportation home; but he went in with his regiment the same as though they were still in the service. He was a German, and I do not suppose he knew the importance of reporting; and as it was only a short time later that I had to leave that army, I therefore did not follow it up, and I find no report of Mercer or of the Ninth Illinois; but I think the regimental reports of the Eighty-first Ohio give all these facts. See War Records, volume 38, part 3, page 463, and report Second Brigade, Second Division Sixteenth Army Corps, volume 38, part 3, page 450.

In my address I did not go much into detail, but I have all the data of this battle compiled, and intend some day to put it in shape;

60

but I give you enough so you can, after examining the reports of Blair and the others, make your article historically correct. Most of it is correct and well-stated, but I know you want to get the dates and movements at the left on such an occasion so full that they will stand criticism, as the Battle of Atlanta was the great battle of that campaign.

Your article and many others that I have seen assumes that it was a part of Hardee's Corps that struck Blair's front—that is, his front that was towards Atlanta; but that is not so. Cleburn's Division was the left Division of Hardee's Corps. There were three other Divisions. Maney's (Cheatham's old Division), Bate's, and Walker's. Walker was the next to Cleburn and attacked Fuller. Bate and Maney struck Sweeney. Cleburn's Division was in front of Blair after Cleburn had driven back his left and he had refused it from Leggett's Hill towards my right. What saved Blair was that Cheatham, who commanded Hood's old Corps, whose orders were to attack Blair's front at the same time Hardee struck his rear, in accordance with the plans of both Hood and Hardee, did not attack because Hardee struck me, which was a surprise to them as well as to me, and when Cheatham got ready to attack Blair's front, hitting Leggett's Division, and on down the Fifteenth Corps, two Divisions, Bate's and Walker's, had been whipped, and were virtually out of the fight, because after the third attack upon me, and my breaking up of one of their columns so badly, they did not come again in any force. They went back to the road on the ridge, just south of and parallel to my line. I forget the name of the road, but it was the one that led off to Decatur, and there they intrenched, and when I pushed forward my skirmishers I found [Pg 58] them in force. Between 3 and 4 o'clock Maney's Division left my front and went around to help Cleburn.

There have also been many statements that in the first attack two Divisions of Hardee's Corps struck the Sixteenth Corps and two the Seventeenth, Blair's. This is not correct. Three Divisions struck my Corps, and one Division, Cleburn's, struck Blair's Corps, and caught his left and rear; but after the third attack on my front Maney's Division was sent around to join Cleburn, and joined in the fiercest attack of the day, about 4 p. m., upon Leggett's and Smith's Divisions after their line had been refused and formed almost at right angles at Leggett's Hill, and reaching out towards me, with Waglin's Brigade on their left. From all accounts this attack was a fearful one, Maney's men reaching and holding the outside of the intrenchments that were occupied by Blair's men. This line faced almost due south, and both forces fought there off and on until about 7 p. m., some of the enemy remaining in the outside intrenchments until Mercer's Brigade of the Sixteenth Corps went in at near midnight to support that line.

Again, many records have it that Blair was forced back early in the battle. This is a mistake, as his Fourth Division, commanded by General Giles A. Smith, which was on the extreme left, held most of his original intrenched line until between 3 and 4 o'clock, when the attack of Cheatham from the Atlanta side forced them to take a new position to keep them from being crushed by Cleburn in the rear and Cheatham's attack from the Atlanta front.

There is another thing that does not seem to be fully understood, and that is that when Blair got his left refused so as to face Maney and Cleburn in his front they were unable to gain any headway on him in their attacks. In fact, they suffered great loss, and they only damaged Blair when they got in behind his left. Blair had three Regiments there refused at right angles to his front, and it was a portion of two of these Regiments that Cleburn picked up. Blair lost nearly all his prisoners from Giles A. Smith's Division, when Cleburn swept down through the gap and got right in behind them before they knew anybody was on them. In fact, Blair's men had to turn around and fight towards their rear, and, as I have stated, Cleburn got past Fuller's right and commenced shooting into his flank. Just after Walker was killed there was a lull, and Fuller turned two regiments right into Cleburn's main line, and, as Captain Allen of the Signal Corps, says, and my records [Pg 59] show, captured that skirmish-line that killed McPherson, and brought it in.

To show McPherson's feeling about Blair's left flank, I sent Fuller's command to that flank the night before on a request from McPherson, who felt anxious about Blair's position, that flank being in the air; but Blair camped Fuller near where he opened the battle in the rear of the Seventeenth Corps instead of connecting his left with it. They camped about a quarter of a mile to his rear and a little back from his extreme left. Blair, no doubt, thought that would protect him, as well as put them in line, but he took one of my batteries (Murray's) and put it in his front line. Now this battery was on the way from Blair to report to me, coming down just as McPherson was going up the road, and the same skirmish-line that killed McPherson killed the horses of that battery and captured a portion of the men, and McPherson really almost fell upon the limber of one of the guns. This was Murray's United States Battery of four pieces. I do not know as I have seen this mentioned in any of the reports, unless it is in mine; but these are the facts of the matter. That is the way a battery of my Corps was reported lost or captured by the enemy. It was passing from Blair to myself, and not captured in line of battle or fighting, as a great many have stated and supposed to be the case.

In your article you speak of Logan taking a part of the Sixteenth Corps and leading it, as though it was right on my front, and then speak of him as leading a portion of the Fifteenth Corps that had been broken through on the Decatur road back into position. The facts are that it was about 4 o'clock in the afternoon when Logan came to me and asked me to send any force I had free to help retake the line that General John C. Brown's Division had broken through the Fifteenth Corps. I sent Mercer's Brigade of the Second Division, and with it sent Captain Jonas of my staff. (See his statement copied in my address.) Logan followed with the command, and it double-quicked the whole distance without stopping. As soon as it got there it found Lightburn's Division drifted back, but holding their line behind the trees, and the enemy in possession of DeGresse's Battery; and as Mercer's Brigade went in on the front, Williamson's Brigade of Wood's Division, which Sherman had directed to make a flank charge, was moving, and they both reached the works together. The men of Mercer's Brigade got hold of DeGresse's guns (see report of Eighty-first Illinois) [Pg 60] and turned them on the enemy. There has always been a contest between these two Brigades as to which got there first, but that does not matter, for they got in together and retook the line. General J. C. Brown, who commanded the Confederate Division, was with me afterwards for many years on the Texas and Pacific Railway, and has given me a full account of his attack, and the fury with which he was forced out by this movement from the flank by Wood and the direct assault by Mercer. Mercer in going in had his horse killed under him.

Fighting along the Fifteenth Corps came late, and was all pretty much after the fighting on my front was over, because when General Logan came to me for aid I was intrenching the new line made by the refusal of Blair's left, and took Mercer's Brigade right out of my front to go with him. The fact is I did not happen to have a single man in reserve. Every man I had on the field was in line from the commencement of the fighting. Sweeney's Division stood right up in the road it was marching on, and the two batteries were in the center of his division; the position was a very strong one. If I had had plenty of time to select a position I could not have found a stronger one. It was the first time I ever saw such execution done by artillery. They used canister against those columns with terrible effect.

To show you how small a thing will sometimes change the prospects in a battle, one of Hardee's Divisions coming towards me got entangled in something—at that time I could not tell what, but on going to the ground afterwards I found that it was a mill-pond—that exposed the flank of Maney's Division that was next to Walker's. Seeing this, I rode down to Mercer and told him to take his Brigade and charge right into it, which he did. It was quite a time before I could tell what the result was, but I soon saw prisoners coming back and knew then that Mercer had them. He had that Division at a great disadvantage, and captured a great many prisoners out of it and several battle-flags. See report Second Brigade, Second Division Sixteenth Army Corps, volume 38, part 3, page 450, Army Records. That charge, no doubt, saved my line, because I had a very thin line, and with the most of Hardee's Corps coming at me in double column, as it was, I have no doubt that if it had reached me it would have given me trouble; but they never got to me on any of their attacks. We were fortunate enough [Pg 61] to break them before they could reach the line, though on Fuller's front they were right up to it when Walker fell.

There was a great dispute between Hood and Hardee about this movement to the rear, Hood claiming that Hardee should have reached there early in the morning, while Hardee claimed he did not receive the order in time to get there before he did—a very fortunate fact for us, for if he had reached the rear of the Seventeenth and Fifteenth Corps, and Cheatham and Stewart had attacked in the front, it would have been rough times for the old Army of the Tennessee; but no doubt they would have come out of it with honor in some way.

I think there is no doubt about the time McPherson was killed—it was just about two hours after the battle had opened. Of course there are all kinds of time given, but the fact of the stopping of the watch of the signal officer, Sheffly, when he fell against the tree at two minutes past two, is almost conclusive evidence. See his statement, volume 11-13, page 242, records Society Army of the Tennessee. You can judge of that yourself, because even before McPherson got up to my right, where he stood, as Strong says, watching me, I had been fighting some time, for he had to ride from near Sherman's headquarters up there, a distance of two to three miles. If you will read carefully the address I am sending you, and the report Blair made—also the address of Strong—I think you will come to the same conclusions I give you. An article on the death of General McPherson, by W. W. Allen, of San Diego, California, Signal Officer of the Army of the Tennessee, appeared in an issue of the National Tribune some time this year, but of what date I do not know. It goes to prove the time and the hour McPherson was killed, and the capture of the skirmish-line that killed him. Of course a great many of the official reports are misleading as to time, and it is only by these circumstances that we can judge definitely. I notice it was 12:20 o'clock, according to Allen, when they first heard the rattle of musketry and artillery.

When you have read Allen's article please return it to me. I will be very glad to give you any further information you may need if it is possible for me to do so.

Truly and cordially yours,
General Green B. Raum.   Grenville M. Dodge.
Chicago, Ill.

[Pg 62]

OLD FORT KEARNEY, NEBRASKA

In the Indian Campaign of 1865.

[Pg 63]

THE INDIAN CAMPAIGNS
1864 AND 1865

Written in 1874
By Major-General Grenville M. Dodge
and Read to the
Colorado Commandery of the Loyal Legion
of the United States, at Denver

April 21, 1907.

In December, 1864, I was assigned to the command of the Department of the Missouri. In January, 1865, I received a dispatch from General Grant asking if a campaign on the plains could be made in the winter. I answered, "Yes, if the proper preparation was made to clothe and bivouac the troops." A few days after I received a dispatch from General Grant ordering me to Fort Leavenworth. In the meantime the Department of Kansas was merged into the Department of the Missouri, placing under my command Missouri, the Indian Territory, Kansas, Colorado, Utah, Wyoming, and all the country south of the Yellowstone River, and embracing all the overland mail-routes and telegraph-lines to the Pacific.

On reaching Port Leavenworth I found that General Curtis, the former commander of that department, had reported against any campaign during the winter; that the Indians had possession of the entire country crossed by the stage-lines, having destroyed the telegraph-lines; and that the people living in Colorado, Utah, California, Western Nebraska and Western Kansas were without mails, and in a state of panic; that the troops distributed along the routes of travel were inside their stockades, the Indians having in nearly every fight defeated them. This success had brought into hostility with the United States nearly every tribe of Indians from Texas on the south to the Yellowstone on the north. It was a formidable combination, and the friendly Indians were daily leaving the reservations to join their hostile brethren. Two thousand Indians [Pg 64] had destroyed over one hundred miles of telegraph, and were in possession of the country between the Arkansas and the North Platte Rivers.

The opinion at Fort Leavenworth before I arrived was that it was impossible to make a successful campaign against these Indians during the winter and successfully open these lines of communication. There were two Regiments of Cavalry in Kansas, mostly idle. There was no communication with any of the posts except by messenger. A dispatch from Colorado showed a panic there, and the people demanded that troops of the Department be stationed there to protect the citizens, instead of their organizing and fighting the Indians, and that martial law had been declared.

I saw, after spending a day at Fort Leavenworth, that it was necessary to change the depressed feeling and temper existing among the troops and the citizens throughout the department. I sent for Bela M. Hughes, agent of the overland stages, and Edward Craighten, general manager and superintendent of the overland telegraph, and consulted fully with them. I selected from my old guides some of the most trusted men, and some of the trusted Indians that I had known, and sent by them to each district commander who could be reached, these two short dispatches:

1. What measures are you taking to keep open the route and protect it? What Indians are engaged in the struggle? Where are their villages? Do their families travel with them? Have you spies in their camps? What action have you taken to repair telegraph-lines? Give me all particulars.

2. Place every mounted man in your command on the South Platte Route. Repair telegraphs; attack any body of Indians you meet, large or small. Stay with them and pound them until they move north of the Platte or south of the Arkansas. I am coming with two Regiments of cavalry to the Platte line and will open and protect it, and whip all the Indians in the way.

I also found that the plains were covered with Indian traders who had permits, under the guise of which they were stealing from the Indians, both friendly and hostile, and were selling them arms and ammunition. I immediately revoked all these permits, and ordered the arrest of all traders who had in their possession Indian or Government stock. I also immediately wired to Major Frank North, who was the interpreter of the Pawnee Indians, and also to the Chief of the Omaha Indians, both of whom had been with me on the plains, and instructed them to select their most trusted men and send them on the plains to ascertain for me the purpose of the hostile Indians, and whether they would head towards the [Pg 65] settlements, or if their movements indicated they would attack only the lines of communication and the trains crossing the plains. At the same time we stopped all trains on the plains and ordered them to the nearest military post, instructing the officers to arm and organize them in companies, and place a United States officer over them, and have them move with the army trains.

Having perfected the preliminary organization for moving upon the stage- and telegraph-lines, we saw it was necessary to concentrate on one line. At this time the stage- and telegraph-lines on the north ran from Fort Leavenworth to Fort Kearney, and from Omaha to Fort Kearney, where they were consolidated, running up the Platte Valley to the mouth of the Lodge Pole, the stage-station at that point being known as Julesburg. The lines here separated again, the main telegraph-line running to old Fort Laramie, thence up the Sweetwater through South Pass and thence to Utah. The stage-line ran up the South Platte to Denver, then by the Cache La Poudre to Laramie Plains, over them to Fort Halleck and Bridger, and on to Utah. I concluded to concentrate all our efforts to open the line from Fort Leavenworth and Omaha to Kearney, thence to Denver and on to Utah, known as the South Platte Route.

The overland route from Fort Leavenworth and Omaha crossing the continent had a stage-station about every twelve miles. The troops along the lines were posted at the forts and stockades about every hundred miles, with a few soldiers distributed at each stage-station. Then scattered along the road were ranches, and relay- and feeding-stations for the regular commercial and supply-trains that were continually on the road. The great mining-camps, and all the inhabitants of Colorado, Utah, Wyoming, and Idaho, were dependent upon these trains for their supplies. In winter these trains were generally mule-trains of twenty wagons each, and during the summer were generally ox-trains of fifty to a hundred wagons each. They were in the habit of straggling along through the country, taking care of themselves. Their stock had to be herded at night, and it was a great temptation to the Indians to steal, and a great deal of this had been done, but no actual fighting or attacking of trains or troops occurred until the winter of 1864-65. The stopping of these trains, mail, and supplies, and the destruction of the telegraph wires, caused great consternation in that country [Pg 66] and on the Pacific Coast, and the demands upon the Government to open and maintain these lines were persistent.

At Fort Leavenworth there appeared to have been no systematic effort to reopen these lines. It seemed that the troops were taking care of the posts and resisting attacks. They did not seem to appreciate the Indian character; that the only way to strengthen and protect the lines of communication was to go for the Indians. What troops had been sent against the Indians were small and weak parties, and had evidently gone out with the intention of locating the Indians and avoiding them.

Along the south emigrant line from Kansas City, following the Arkansas River to New Mexico, was the line of supplies for all of New Mexico and Southern Colorado. The Indians here were in possession. The travel and traffic along it were not to be compared with that along the northern lines. Then again the citizens of Kansas and Nebraska had settled along these routes as far west as the 100th Meridian, obtaining their living from this great traffic, and the Indians in their raids had picked them up, a family at a time, until they had a great many prisoners, mostly women and children, the men being generally massacred when captured.

I found the Eleventh Kansas Cavalry at Fort Riley, and the Sixteenth Kansas Cavalry at Fort Leavenworth, and immediately placed them *en route* for Fort Kearney. All the posts were, unfortunately, short of subsistence, forage, and ammunition. The three-months' Regiments enlisted in Colorado for the Indian service had been discharged, their time having expired, and there had been no troops sent to take their places. My only resource was to utilize the Colorado Militia until I could send troops 600 miles to take their places.

I immediately started for Fort Kearney, taking with me a few soldiers in the stage and one of my staff. It was the opinion of all the officers at Fort Leavenworth that it would be impossible for me to make the trip, but I knew it required personal presence among the troops to bring about quick results. The troops that I had ordered to march from Fort Riley refused to march in the winter. I answered to place under arrest all officers of the companies and Regiments that refused to obey the order, and have them report to Fort Leavenworth, intending to replace them with veteran officers of the department whom I knew would move, no matter what the hardship. The next morning I received a report from [Pg 67] Fort Kiley that the troops would move. The Regiment that marched from Fort Riley to Fort Kearney lost thirteen men from freezing, as the weather was very severe, and while they were properly clothed, they did not know how to protect themselves from the weather.

On my arrival at Fort Kearney I immediately notified Mr. Hughes, agent of the stage-lines, that I was prepared to protect his stages, and called upon him to replace his stock immediately, ready to start out his stages. I also notified Mr. Craighten, superintendent of the telegraph-lines, to replace his operators, for I would have his lines open in a few days. Both of these orders were made known to the public. I also notified the "press" at Omaha and Fort Leavenworth that all trains which were tied up on the plains would be moved to their destinations during that month. We found it necessary to inspire energy and confidence in these three great interests, as not one of them even thought we would succeed, and, in fact, the "press" comments on our orders showed that they had no faith in them. I found on the line of the Platte the Seventh Iowa Cavalry, and at Fort Laramie and on the Sweetwater the Eleventh Ohio Cavalry.

When we arrived in sight of Fort Kearney the troops were prepared to fight us, thinking it was a band of Indians. We discovered that the troops were depressed from the success of the Indians and the murder and mutilation of their comrades, and that they hardly stuck their heads out of the stockade. Having had experience with Indians, I called the troops together and instructed them how to handle and to fight Indians, telling them that an aggressive war would be made against the Indians, and no matter how large the Indian bands were, or how small the troop, that hereafter they must stand and fight; that if they did the Indians would run. If they did not, the Indians would catch and scalp them, and even if they had to retreat, they must do so with their faces to the enemy.

The Indians, after the Chivington fight on Big Sandy, had concentrated upon the South Platte and on the Sweetwater. The reports showed that they held possession from Julesburg to Valley Junction and to Mud Springs, and held the telegraph-line west of Fort Laramie. They had with them 2,000 head of captured stock and had captured all the stage-stations and many trains, devastated the ranches, butchered many men, women, and children, and destroyed 100 miles of telegraph.

[Pg 68] To show more plainly than I can describe the condition of the country, I give the reports of the three commanding officers along the South Platte Route, in answer to the dispatches which I sent by messenger to all commanders the day I arrived at Fort Leavenworth. These answers met me at Fort Kearney.

General Robert Mitchell, who commanded the territory from Omaha to Lodge Pole, replied as follows:

The telegraph from Lodge Pole Creek, twenty-five miles west to Julesburg, on Laramie Route, is destroyed for fifteen miles. Poles cut down and destroyed on the Denver line beyond Julesburg for the first fifty miles. The telegraph is destroyed about ten miles north. We are compelled to haul poles from 130 to 140 miles. Every means in my power is used to have the lines fixed. All the available troops I have at my disposal are in the vicinity of Julesburg, except some small garrisons at posts required to be kept up on the Denver route. My district only extends to Julesburg. I have sent some troops, however, up that route fifty miles since the outbreaks and find everything destroyed. We have no communication with Denver, and have not had since the last outbreak. Neither can I communicate with Fort Laramie in consequence of the lines being down. I have been traversing the country constantly on and adjacent to the mail- and telegraph-lines during the past four months, sending guards on the stages, and, when deemed necessary, mounted guards and patrols on all dangerous portions of the road through my district.

This plan succeeded until an overpowering force attacked Julesburg and drove the troops inside of their works and burned the stage- and telegraph-station, destroying a large amount of stores for both companies. The overland stage cannot run through until they can provide for supplies for stock from Julesburg to the Junction, where overland stage leaves Denver route, everything belonging to the stage company, citizens and government being entirely destroyed. The Indian villages are unknown to us. From the best information I have I believe them to be on the Powder River. I know certainly there is a large village there. There have been no squaws in the country, to my knowledge, since last fall. The tribes engaged are the Cheyennes, Arapahoes, Kiowas, Brule, Ogallala Sioux, a portion of the Blackfeet, and a large portion of what is known as the Missouri River Sioux, the same Indians General Sully made the campaign against last summer. From 3,000 to 5,000 additional troops will be needed to punish the Indians. One column will never be able to overtake them, unless they are willing to give battle. I think three columns of men, 1,000 strong each, with ample garrison on the overland-mail and telegraph lines, well mounted and supplied, can clear out the country of all hostile Indians, if done before grass comes. After that time, in my judgment, it will take twice that number of men.

In addition to the troubles west, I would not be surprised any day to hear of an outbreak in the northern part of my district. I am informed by Indian scouts that there is a large encampment of Indians on the Running Water that are ready to engage in the war against the whites. Among them are some of the Yanktonais Sioux.

Colonel R. R. Livingston reported as follows:

In reply to your inquiries I would respectfully state that in the early part of January last, indications of large parties of Indians moving westward on Republican were reported by the scouts sent to gain information of their movements. On January 7th they had crossed South Fork of Platte River, twenty-three miles west of this post, camped with their families, forming a camp of 400 lodges, containing eight warriors each, many lodges being [Pg 69] thirty robes in size. They commenced the work of destruction along the road west as far as Junction Station, 100 miles from here. Their forces in this fight were not less than 2,000, well armed with breech-loading carbines and rifles. A desperate attempt on their part to burn the overland-stage station near this post was made at this time, but was frustrated by the gallantry of Captain N. J. O'Brien, Company F, Seventh Iowa Cavalry. Every ranch and stage-station from Junction Station to this post is burned, and the charred remains of every inmate who failed to escape tells of the brutality they were subjected to. I telegraphed Hon. Sam H. Elbert, acting Governor of Colorado, early in January of the state of things. The troops of Colorado have been withdrawn from Valley, fifty miles west of here, I surmise, to concentrate around Denver. The telegraph-lines to Salt Lake and the Denver branch lines are destroyed for a distance of nearly ten miles on the northern route, and in different points throughout 100 miles along the Denver route.

I have but 360 troops, but so long as human endurance holds out we will work night and day to get the communication perfect with the west.

The Indians engaged in this war are the Cheyennes, Ogallalas, and Brule Sioux. They have gone northward towards Horse Creek and Fort Laramie. Their trail leads in that direction, but they are slow in marching, feeling audacious and indifferent to any effort from the small body of troops in this district. I saw their signals today, probably those of small war parties, on the North Platte. You will hear of continued murders and robberies as long as the road is so poorly protected by troops. No spies can be used now, owing to numerous small war parties being met everywhere in this country. I predict that if more troops are not sent into this district immediately, this road will be stripped of every ranch and white man on it. Should these Indians swing around by Niobrara River and take the Omaha road below Kearney, where settlements are numerous, infinite mischief will result to the settlers. What we need are troops, supplies for them, and a vigorous campaign against these hostile Indians. They must be put on the defensive instead of us. No difficulty can arise in finding them. Over 2,000 cattle accompany them.

Headquarters, District Colorado.
Denver, Colorado Territory, Feb. 2, 1865.

The Indians are bold in the extreme. They have burned every ranch between Julesburg and Valley Station, and nearly all the property at latter place; driven off all stock, both public and private. These Indians are led by white men, and have complete control of all the country outside my district, so that I am hemmed in.

The weather has been very severe here for nearly three weeks; the thermometer 30 degrees below zero, with quite a fall of snow on the ground. I have tried every means in my power to raise volunteers for three months' State service, but as yet have not succeeded, owing to the factional spirit existing in the community.

The Legislature took the matter in hand at my suggestion, appropriating so much money. Territorial bonds, to give the men a bounty and purchase horses to mount them on, as I have none; but the members cannot agree on the spoil likely in their estimation to accrue from such a proceeding, so the bill has not yet passed. I addressed the Speaker of the House yesterday, informing him that unless something was done within forty-eight hours I would be compelled, much against my will, to proclaim martial law and stop all business, forcing every man to enter the ranks and open the line of communication. I have now a city organization of about 100 men organized into companies, so that in case of an attack here I would have something tangible to lay hold of and make a fight. I have had a great deal of trouble in this matter, as there is no concert of action, every man suspecting his fellow of some chicanery.

[Pg 70] Fort Lyon is being rapidly fortified, so that 200 men can defend it against 2,000 Indians. Militia companies are being organized all over the settled parts of the country (under penalty of being pressed into service) to defend the frontier settlements southward, and could I but get a Regiment here now I could keep things in a running trim until the arrival of a sufficient force to make a campaign. The Indians are now determined to make it a war of extermination, and nothing short of 5,000 men can make it extermination for them.

Major Wynkoop informed me from Fort Lyon that many warriors were on the headwaters of the Smoky Hill and intended attacking all the settlements as well as Denver. Provisions, owing to the transportation-line being cut off, are at an exorbitant price, as well as labor and forage.

Cannot troops be sent out here immediately, or authority to raise companies, which could be easily done, for one year?

The Santa Fe line has threatened to stop running on account of the Indians. Should such be the case, then all is cut off.

Respectfully, your obedient servant,
Thomas Moonlight,
Colonel Eleventh Kansas Cavalry, Commanding.

Colonel Chivington, from Fort Rankin, reported:

Lieutenant-Colonel Collins, with 200 men of the Eleventh Ohio, and Company D, Seventh Iowa Cavalry, fought Indians from the 4th to the 9th inst., at Mud Springs. The Indians at one time charged our forces in the face of artillery and were nearly successful. Two thousand warriors were engaged in the fight. It is supposed forty Indians were killed. Beaure's and Craighten's herds were driven off. The Indians crossed at Bush Creek, going north. The telegraph poles were gone and wires so inextricably tangled as to be useless. Seven hundred lodges crossed Pole Creek, six miles below Pole Creek crossing.

These Indians were not driven off and the telegraph-lines retaken without severe fighting and loss of many soldiers. Within two weeks the troops drove these Indians north, where a detachment of troops from Fort Laramie attacked them and drove them across the Platte. Finally the Indians saw that a different warfare was being made against them, and they fled to their villages on the Powder River and in the Black Hills country.

There was such energy and such spirit displayed by the troops, that after two weeks' work they had the telegraph-lines replaced between Omaha and Denver, a distance of 600 miles, and this without any additional force to aid them. The progress made in putting up the wires is shown by this report:

My troop is at Moore's ranch; passed there at 2 o'clock. We ran twelve miles of wire and set eight miles of poles, had two severe fights, and marched fifty-five miles in fifty-two hours. Operators furnished valuable service.

E. B. Murphy,
Captain Seventh Iowa Cavalry.

The thermometers all this time were from 5 to 10 degrees below zero. On February 13th telegraphic communication was [Pg 71] resumed through to California, and Mr. Craighten notified the Government of the fact.

An inquiry made of Craighten by General Grant, as to where I was located (Craighten being a personal friend of mine who was most skeptical at the start of my accomplishing anything with the material I had, was overjoyed at our success), was answered, "Nobody knows where he is, but everybody knows where he has been."

From the 5th to the 13th of February every mounted man on that line was in the saddle, either assisting the operators or chasing real or imaginary Indians. The moment a scout came in, instructions were given to the officers to send them out and not allow any mounted troops in the stockade until the lines were opened and the Indians driven at least 100 miles away from the line of telegraph, and the only dashes the Indians made after we got fairly at them was to cut off a part of an unguarded train, and at unguarded ranches, and at those stage-stations where only a few soldiers were located; but in every attack the soldiers stood their ground and fought, and when driven they only backed far enough to get a secure place. The troops knew better than to go back to the fortified posts, as they had instructions to keep to the hills, but in nearly every case they were successful, and the daring that some of the troops showed in these fights was remarkable.

Great atrocities were committed by the Indians, scalping the men alive and abusing the women. This caused the troops to stand and fight, preferring to die rather than to fall into their hands. Wherever a fight was successfully made, no matter whether commissioned or non-commissioned officers commanded, I telegraphed him in person thanking him, and to the commanding officer of his Regiment, requesting that he be given the first promotion, and wrote to the Governor of his State.

As soon as this stage-line was opened we concentrated about 500 mounted men, intending to catch the Indians before they left the North Platte; but the Indians fled as soon as they heard of this, and did not stop until they reached Powder River, too far north for us to follow until arrangements were made for supplies for troops and stock, as everything had to be teamed from Fort Leavenworth.

The storms during March were very severe. Snow lay two feet on the level and was crusted so hard that for weeks it was almost impossible to force animals through it. As soon as we heard from my scouts of the departure of the Indians and found they had no [Pg 72] intention of molesting the citizens of Nebraska, and had placed themselves on Powder River too far north to return until the return of the grass in May, I distributed the troops along the stage- and telegraph-lines to Salt Lake, and returned to open the South Route to New Mexico.

My experience on the North Route, with the reports from the troops and from my Indians, soon satisfied me that every Indian tribe of any importance from the British Possessions in the north to the Red River in the south, were preparing to engage in open hostilities. These tribes often pretended to be friendly, deceiving the Government and the Indian agent, a crafty trick that was impossible to make the Government understand. For instance, they would go to the Indian agent for provisions, and would make him believe that they were for peace, and would promise to bring to the agency their tribe. Probably by the time the report of the Indian agent reached the Government, this same tribe would be off on the warpath and have captured a train or murdered some settlers, and the troops in return had attacked and destroyed them, and we were called to account for it, as it was claimed by the agents we were attacking peaceable Indians. This went so far that it prevented me from opening the southern emigrant trail several weeks. Finally I took the matter in my own hands, regardless of the action or report of the agents.

While these parleys were going on the Indians suddenly appeared all along the southern emigrant trail in the Arkansas River Valley, attacking trains, posts, and escorts. I threw my troops against the bands of Southern Arapahoes, Cheyennes, Comanches, and Kiowas that were in the vicinity of the trail. The troops had caught on to the severe fighting on the Platte, had heard of the new methods of warfare and victories, and they in all cases stood their ground and defeated the Indians, although they suffered severely in some instances. This was a reception that the Indians did not expect and they fled to the Wichita Mountains, suing for peace, which I knew was simply to prevent us attacking them there, but accomplished its purpose with the Government and finally brought about the treaties that were not worth the paper they were written on, and later on forced the campaigns that Sheridan afterwards made, while if we had been allowed to have followed them up and punish them as we did the northern tribes, we would have conquered a peace that would have been a lasting one.

[Pg 73] The Indians of the plains are the best skirmishers in the world. In rapidity of movements, in perfect horsemanship, sudden whirling, protecting the body by clinging to the side of the horse, and rapid movements in open and difficult ground, no trained cavalry in the world can equal them. On foot their ability to hide behind any obstruction, in ravine, along creeks, and under creek and river banks, and in fighting in the open plains or level ground, the faculty to disappear is beyond one's belief except he has experienced it. In skulking and sharpshooting they are adepts, but troops properly instructed are a match for them on foot, and never fail to drive and route them, if they will stand and fight and never retreat except slowly with their faces to them. I have seen several times, when caught in a tight place, bands of Indians held by a few men by holding to ridges and slowly retreating, always using our rifles at every opportunity when an Indian was in range, never wasting a shot on them unless there was a probability of hitting them. The Indians have a mortal fear of such tactics.

In a fight the Indians will select the positions and pick out quickly any vantage ground, and sometimes as high as 200 will concentrate at such a point where we could not concentrate twenty men without exposing them, and from this vantage ground they will pour a deadly fire on the troops, and we cannot see an Indian—only puffs of smoke. By such tactics as this they harass and defeat our troops. Many a fight occurred between Indians and soldiers both watching the smoke to show each other's position. You can watch this kind of a fight and never see a person unless some one is hit and exposes himself, when it is nearly always a sure death. The Indian character is such that he will not stand continual following, pounding, and attacking. Their life and methods are not accustomed to it, and the Indians can be driven by very inferior forces by continually watching, attacking, and following. None of our campaigns have been successful that have not been prepared to follow the Indians day and night, attacking them at every opportunity until they are worn out, disbanded, or forced to surrender, which is the sure result of such a campaign.

The Indians during the months they had been hostile, and especially in their attacks on the stage-stations and ranches, had captured a large number of men, women, and children. These prisoners had made known to the troops, by dropping notes along the trail and through the reports of friendly Indians, their terrible [Pg 74] condition and the usage that was being made of them. Their appeals to us to rescue them were pitiful.

I knew the prisoners would be sent far north to the villages, and their winter quarters out of our reach; that these villages were unprotected because every brave and dog-soldier had his warpaint on and was joining the hostile forces attacking along our lines, which were increasing every day. I also knew it would be impossible for any of our troops to reach them or to rescue them by following them, and as soon as I arrived at Fort Kearney I asked authority of the Government to enlist and muster into service two companies of Pawnee Indians, to be under the command of their old interpreter, Major North, who I knew to be a brave, level-headed leader. This authority was immediately given me, and Major North was given confidential instructions to proceed to the Sioux country, apparently on scout duty, but to watch his opportunity and rescue these prisoners, while their braves were down fighting us. He started, but storms of snow came down so heavy that his ponies could get nothing to eat, and during the latter part of February and all of March these storms were continuous, the snow falling to the depth of two feet over the entire plains. Major North was compelled to seek shelter in the river bottoms, and browsed his stock on cottonwood limbs to save them. In the campaign of the summer and winter of 1865 and 1866 Major North, with his two enlisted companies, to which I added two more, made some wonderful marches, scouts, battles, and captures, and during that campaign we recaptured and had surrendered to us many of these women and children prisoners.

After the war Major North became manager of the Indians in Buffalo Bill's Wild West Show, and died in that service. He was a noted man on the plains. My acquaintance with him commenced in 1856, and together we had seen and endured many hardships. It was seldom one met his equal in any of the different phases of plains life. Although he had led an eventful career, still I never heard him refer to what he had done or accomplished, or the part he had taken in battles, and probably no man was ever more worshiped than he was by the two tribes of Pawnee Indians; and his death was virtually their destruction, for during his life among them he held them

80

under good discipline and kept them away from vice, diseases, and war.

[Pg 75] A great many amusing reports came to me from my scouts and the captured Indians. When on the plains in the 50's I was known among the Indians by the name, in their language, that signified "Long Eye," "Sharp Eye," and "Hawk Eye." This came from the fact that when I first went among them it was as an engineer making surveys through their country. With my engineering instruments I could set a head-flag two or three miles away, even further than an Indian could see, and it is their custom to give a practical name to everything. Of course I was not many days on the plains until it reached the Indians that "Long Eye" was there, and in every fight that occurred they had me present. They said I could shoot as far as I could see. The scouts said the Indian chiefs laid their defeats to that fact. Then again they were very superstitious about my power in other matters. When the overland telegraph was built they were taught to respect it and not destroy it. They were made to believe that it was a Great Medicine. This was done after the line was opened to Fort Laramie by stationing several of their most intelligent chiefs at Fort Laramie and others at Fort Kearney, the two posts being 300 miles apart, and then having them talk to each other over the wire and note the time sent and received. Then we had them mount their fleetest horses and ride as fast as they could until they met at Old Jule's ranch, at the mouth of the Lodge Pole, this being about half way between Kearney and Laramie. Of course this was astonishing and mysterious to the Indians. Thereafter you could often see Indians with their heads against the telegraph poles, listening to the peculiar sound the wind makes as it runs along the wires and through the insulators. It is a soughing, singing sound. They thought and said it was "Big Medicine" talking. I never could convince them that I could not go to the telegraph poles the same as they did and tell them what was said, or send a message for them to some chief far away, as they had often seen me use my traveling-instrument and cut into the line, sending and receiving messages. Then again, most of the noted scouts of the plains who had married into the different tribes had been guides for me, and many of these men were half-breeds, and were with these hostile Indians. Some of them took part with them, but more of them had tried to pacify and bring them to terms, and they gave me information about those who were not engaged in the depredations.

[Pg 76] I was supposed to be, by the Indians of the plains, a person of great power and great moment. These half-breeds worked upon their superstitions, endeavoring to convince them it was useless to fight "Long Eye." No doubt my appearing on the plains the time I did, and the fact that from the time I appeared until the time I left, the troops had nothing but success, carried great weight with them, and seemed to confirm what the old voyageurs and guides told them, and had much influence in causing their abandonment of the Platte country and returning to their villages.

My own experience on the plains led me to be just as watchful and just as vigilant when I knew the Indians were not near me as I was when they were in sight. In all my travels I never allowed them to camp near or occupy my camps even in the time of peace, when they were friendly, and I never allowed myself to knowingly do them an injustice, making it a point never to lie to them in any of my councils and treaties, or never allow, if I knew it, the interpreter to deceive them. That brought me respect in all my dealings with them, and I treated them with respect, courtesy, and consideration, and demanded the same from them. This, no doubt, was one of the principal reasons that in fifteen years, more or less, of intercourse with them, traveling through their country both during the times they were hostile and at peace, that I escaped many of the misfortunes that befell others.

Although this short campaign was not remarkable for great battles or large loss by killed and wounded, still it required great fortitude from the troops, and often great personal courage, and its success was of great moment to the Government and to the people of the plains and the Pacific Coast, for over these three great overland routes were carried the mails, telegrams, and traffic during the entire war of the rebellion, which did much to hold these people loyal to our Government. A long stoppage was a destruction to business, and would bring starvation and untold misery; and when, with only thirteen days and nights of untiring energy on the part of the troops in a winter of unheard-of severity, California, Utah and Colorado were put in communication with the rest of the world, there was great rejoicing. In seventeen days the stages were started and overland travel was again safe, after being interrupted for two months, and by March 1st the commercial [Pg 77] trains were all *en route* to their destinations and I had returned to my duties at the headquarters of the Department, in St. Louis.

It was with no little satisfaction that I answered a personal letter General Grant had written me, when he assigned me to this duty, and which I found awaiting me on my return to Fort Leavenworth. In his letter he outlined what it was necessary to do and why he had asked me to take the field. He judged rightly of the condition of affairs and the necessity of immediate action. I wrote him how promptly the troops responded to my call. They had opened the overland routes; they had made them secure and were then guarding them, and they would be kept open. But after grass came, unless these hostile Indians were thoroughly chastised, they would certainly and successfully attack them and prevent safe travel overland, and from my letter the order soon came for me to prepare for the extensive campaign of the next summer and winter that followed these Indians to the Yellowstone on the north and the Cimarron on the south, and conquered a peace with every hostile tribe.

[Pg 78]

JAMES BRIDGER

Chief Guide to Indian Campaign, 1865-6.

[Pg 79]

THE INDIAN CAMPAIGNS
1865 AND 1866

During the Indian campaigns of the winter and spring of 1864-65, against the Indians that were holding all the overland roads, stations, telegraph and emigrant routes over the plains, my command reopened them in a short campaign of sixty days in which many fights occurred in which the troops were uniformly successful. The telegraph-lines were rebuilt, the stages re-established, the mails transported regularly, and protection given. Although we were able to drive the Indians off of all of these routes and open them successfully and hold them open, my experience convinced me that as soon as grass started on the plains these Indians would again come down on the routes, and that the only possible way of settling the Indian question was to make a well-planned and continuous campaign against them on the Arkansas, the Smoky Hill, the Republican, and the North and South Platte Valley routes, and to keep them off the traveled roads. To do this we would be obliged to get our troops into their country as soon as possible and go for their villages.

In my report to the Government, in April, 1865, I set forth the necessity for this and outlined the plans. Upon the receipt of that report I received authority from General Grant and General Pope to go forward and carry out the plans that I had suggested. This plan contemplated placing upon the plains about 5,000 men to protect the stations and telegraph-lines, furnish escort to emigrants and Government trains of supplies that were necessary to supply the wants of that vast country with provisions and outfit five movable columns of soldiers, a total of 6,000 or 7,000 men. Contracts were immediately made for the supplies for this number of men; for horses for the cavalry, and for the supplying of the posts on the plains with a surplus at each, so that if the campaign extended into the winter it would not have to stop for want of provisions. The campaign in the spring had to be made on supplies moved there in the middle of winter, at great cost and suffering. [Pg 80] The Quartermaster and Commissary at Fort Leavenworth made contracts for supplies to be delivered in June, and General Grant sent to Fort Leavenworth something like 10,000 troops, very few of whom got into the campaigns from the fact that the troops would no sooner reach Fort Leavenworth than they would protest, claiming that the Civil War was ended and saying they had not enlisted to fight Indians. The Governors of their States, Congressmen, and other influential men, would bring such pressure to bear that the War Department would order them mustered out. While the Government was at great expense in moving these troops to the plains, some even reaching as far as Julesburg, we never got any service from them; they were a great detriment, and caused much delay in our plans, so that the overland routes had to be protected by about one-half of the troops that it was at first thought necessary to accomplish the work. Three Regiments of infantry, eleven Regiments of cavalry, and three Batteries of artillery, that reported to me under the order of General Grant, were mustered out on the march between Fort Leavenworth and Julesburg.

There was enlisted for the Indian campaign, five Regiments of United States volunteers, recruited from the rebel prisoners, who, desiring to be at liberty, were willing to enlist under the United States flag to fight Indians, and these five Regiments had to be depended upon mostly for taking care of all the country west of the Lakes,—the overland routes on the plains, to man the posts on the upper Missouri and Mississippi Rivers, and for escorts for surveying parties, etc. So when I was ready to move all five columns I had less than 7,000 officers and men in my department. The Indians commenced their depredations on all the routes in April, especially on the Arkansas route, where we had to contend with the South Cheyennes, Comanches, Apaches, Kiowas, and Arapahoe tribes. This district was under the command of Brigadier-General Ford, a very efficient officer, and it was planned that he should make a campaign in May and June into the Indian country, crossing the Arkansas and moving south for their villages, which we knew were situated in the Wichita Mountains. General Ford had a compact veteran command, and fought one or two battles before crossing the Arkansas. Just about the time he was ready to cross the Arkansas the Government sent west a peace commission composed of Senator Doolittle, General Alex McD. McCook, and others. The Indian agent for these tribes was Colonel J. H. Leavenworth. [Pg 81] They no sooner reached the Indian country than they protested against the movement of any troops into the territory south of the Arkansas River. In fact, General McCook issued an order, using General Pope's name as authority, stopping General Ford's movement. He had no authority to do this, but General Ford obeyed, as the information came to him that these chiefs were assembling at the mouth of the Little Arkansas to make peace. After parleying with the Indians, the commission accomplished nothing, and the Indians all the time were committing their depredations on the emigrant trains that were passing up the Arkansas Valley to New Mexico and Colorado. All the protests and appeals of General Pope, General Ford and myself to the Government in relation to this matter seemed to have no effect. These Indians had murdered the settlers, wiped out their ranches, and stolen their property and their stock, and our scouts who went among them saw their captures in plenty. As soon as we would start out to punish them, even those that had crossed north of the Arkansas River, protests were sent to Washington and came back to us, so that we virtually accomplished nothing. The condition of matters became so complicated that on June 6, 1865, I stated my views of the question to Major-General John Pope, commanding the Military Division of the Missouri, as follows:

Headquarters Department of the Missouri.
Fort Leavenworth, June 6, 1865.

Major-General John Pope, Commanding Military Division of the Missouri:

General: You have been notified of the action of Major-General McCook, under the orders of the Congressional Committee, in stopping the expedition of General Ford south of the Arkansas, that they might confer, and, if possible, make peace with the Arapahoes, Cheyennes, Comanches, Kiowas, etc. Colonel Leavenworth started south a week ago to bring the chiefs up to the mouth of Cow Creek, and while we are endeavoring to make terms with them, their warriors are strung along the route from Zarah to Lyon, dashing in on any train that they find off its guard. They are in parties of from fifteen to fifty, and hide in the valleys and ravines. These Indians now have their villages at Fort Cobb, and have driven out all friendly Indians and traders, declaring that they mean war and nothing else. They are composed of one band of Arapahoes, led by Little Rover; one small band of Cheyennes, three bands of Apaches, a large body of Comanches, also the Southern Comanches, and all the Kiowas, and they have no respect for our authority or power, and I have no faith in any peace made by them until they are made to feel our strength. I do not believe it will be a month before we hear of large trains being captured or attacked by them in force. They notified Jesus, the Mexican trader sent in by General Carleton, to leave, and it is said they murdered Major Morrison, a trader permitted to go in by General Carleton. It appeared to me bad policy to give permits to any of the traders to go among them to trade. Not one of them will act as guide to take a force toward them.

[Pg 82] Colonel Leavenworth satisfied the committee, and I think General McCook also, that the Comanches and others had not committed any depredations. There is not an officer or trader who has been on the plains but knows they have been in all or nearly all the outrages committed. I desire very much to have peace with the Indians, but I do think we should punish them for what they have done, and that they should feel our power and have respect for us. My plan to reach them is to start in three columns for Fort Cobb; viz., First, by Major Merrill's route; second, by Captain Booner's route; third, from the mouth of Mulberry Creek, on the Arkansas. Make the parties about 400 or 500 strong, and march direct for their villages. This will draw every warrior after us and leave the Santa Fe route free. When we get down there if the Indians are so anxious for peace, they will have an opportunity to show it, and we can make an agreement with them that will stop hostilities until the properly authorized authorities conclude a lasting peace. I have attempted to get these expeditions off twice. The first time they were stopped by General Halleck, on Colonel Leavenworth's representations. He started to make peace; the Indians stole all his stock, and very nearly got his scalp. He came back for fight and wished to whip them, but has now changed again, and it is possible he may get the chiefs together, but I very much doubt it; and, even if he does, they will only represent a portion of each tribe. I have concluded, by representations of the Congressional Committee made to General Ford, to wait and see the effects of Colonel Leavenworth's mission. I will have my troops at the designated points. If he should fail I will go forward and make the campaign as originally ordered. I desire to add that there is not a leading officer on the plains who has had any experience with Indians who has faith in peace made with any of these Indians unless they are punished for the murders, robberies and outrages they have committed for over a year; and unless we have a settled policy, either fight and allow the commanding officer of the department to dictate terms of peace to them, or else it be decided that we are not to fight, but make some kind of peace at all hazards, we will squander the summer without result. Indians will rob and murder, and some Indian agents will defend them, and when fall comes I will be held responsible for not having protected the route or punished them for what they may have done. It must be evident to the Government that I cannot be making war on the Indians while other parties are at the same time making peace, as has been the case so far. Whatever may be the desire of the Government, I will lend all my energies to carry it out and make every officer and man under me do the same. I cannot approve the manner in which the Indians have been treated, and have no faith in them, nor will I allow such treatment as shown at the Big Sandy fight. If peace is concluded I trust that their reservations may be made at safe distances from overland routes so far as possible, and that they be made to keep away from them.

I am, very respectfully, your obedient servant,
G. M. Dodge,
Major-General.

The Government, after receiving General Pope's and my own views, sent out Inspector-General D. B. Sackett, of the Regular Army, to investigate the conditions in that country and to report to the Government the actual facts. In the meantime the peace commission that had been endeavoring to negotiate with these Indians had gone on to Denver, still protesting against any movement against the Indians, believing that peace could be brought about. General Sackett, upon reaching the Indian country, sent [Pg 83] the following dispatch, on June 14, 1865, to the commanding officer at Fort Larned, Kas.:

For the last few days the Indians along the route have been very active and hostile; many men have been murdered, hundreds of animals have been stolen, Fort Dodge has lost every animal. The force can now do nothing with the Indians. A large and effective cavalry force under a good commander must be sent here without delay, or the large number of trains now on the plains will be destroyed or captured.

Upon the receipt of this dispatch I immediately gave orders to the commanding officer to go out and concentrate our forces north of the Arkansas, and to protect the trains, but not to go south of the river. This they accomplished very effectively, and drove all the Indians south of the Arkansas, killing and capturing a good many. On June 14th, General Pope wrote a long letter to General U. S. Grant, enclosing my letter to him, reiterating what I had said, and insisting for very strong reasons that the Indians should be left entirely to the military; that there should be no peace commission sent until the military had met these Indians and brought them to terms, either by fighting or negotiations; and afterwards for the commission to go there and make such arrangements as they saw proper. In the mustering out of troops General Ford was relieved of the command and Major-General John B. Sanborn, a very efficient officer, was sent to take his place. It was now agreed that after the failure of the peace commission to accomplish anything with these Indians that I should make the campaigns south of the Arkansas, and General Sanborn concentrated his troops and moved to the Arkansas. Before I reached there I received a communication from Colonel Leavenworth stating that all the chiefs of the Indians were then on Cow Creek, anxious to meet him. At the same time, a dispatch came from Washington to General Pope, stopping Sanborn's movement. General Pope immediately arranged to have an interview with these Indians, and General Sanborn went there with instructions to make an agreement with them that they should keep off of the overland trails, and to arrange a time for a commission to meet them, later in the year. On August 5th Sanborn agreed with the chiefs of the Kiowas, Apaches, Comanches, and Arapahoes, on the part of the Government, to suspend all actions of hostility towards any of the tribes above mentioned and to remain at peace until the fourth day of October, 1865, when they were to meet the Government commissioners at Bluffs Creek about forty miles south [Pg 84] of the Little Arkansas. This agreement did not take in the South Cheyennes, who had been more mischievous than any of the tribes, but this tribe kept south of the Arkansas, retaining all the stock they captured, and none of them were punished for the murders they committed. It was a business matter on their part to remain at peace only until the troops moved out of that country and to prevent Sanborn with his organized forces from going south to their villages and punishing them. The effect of this agreement was that the Indians continued their depredations through the following years,—not so much by killing but by stealing,—until finally they became so hostile that in the campaign against them by General Sheridan, in 1868, an agreement was made with them forcing all the tribes to move into the Indian Territory. If General Ford or General Sanborn had been allowed to go forward and punish these Indians as they deserved, they would have been able to make not only a peace, but could have forced them to go on the reservation in the Indian territories, and thus have saved the murders and crimes that they committed for so many years afterwards; however, this agreement of Sanborn's allowed the emigration to go forward over the Arkansas, properly organized and guarded, and it was not molested during the rest of that year.

To show the conditions on the overland routes up the two forks of the Platte River at the time, I sent this dispatch:

Headquarters Department of the Missouri.
St. Louis, Mo., June 17, 1865.

Major-General John Pope, Commanding Military Division of the Missouri, St. Louis:

General: There is no doubt but that all, or nearly all, the tribes of Indians east of the Rocky Mountains from the British Possessions on the north to the Red River on the south are engaged in open hostilities against the Government. It is possible that in a few of the tribes there are some chiefs and warriors who desire to be friendly, but each day reduces the number of these, and they even are used by the hostile tribes to deceive us as to their intentions and keep us quiet. The Crows and Snakes appear to be friendly, but everything indicates that they too are ready to join in the hostilities, and the latter (the Snakes) are accused of being concerned in the depredations west of the mountains. In my opinion there is but one way to effectually terminate these Indian troubles; viz., to push our cavalry into the heart of their country from all directions, to punish them whenever and wherever we find them, and force them to respect our power and to sue for peace. Then let the military authorities make informal treaties with them for a cessation of hostilities. This we can accomplish successfully, for the Indians will treat with soldiers, as they fear them and have confidence in their word. Any treaty made now by civilians, Indian agents, or others, will, in my opinion, amount to nothing, as the Indians in all the tribes openly express dissatisfaction with them and contempt for them. The friendly Indians say that whenever the hostile bands are made [Pg 85] aware of our ability and determination to whip them, they will readily and in good faith treat with our officers and comply with any demands we may make. If we can keep citizen agents and traders from among them we can, I am confident, settle the matter this season, and when settled I am clearly of the opinion that these Indians should be dealt with entirely by competent commissioned officers of the Army, whom they will respect and who will not only have the power to make them comply with the terms of the agreements made, but will also have the power and authority to compel troops, citizens and others to respect implicitly and to comply strictly with the obligations assumed on our part. The cavalry now moving into the Indian country will, I doubt not, if allowed to proceed and carry out the instructions given them, accomplish the object designed by bringing about an effectual peace and permanent settlement of our Indian difficulties.

I am, General, very respectfully, your obedient servant,
G. M. Dodge,
Major-General.

The campaign to the north was planned with a view of going after all the northern Indians then at war — the Arapahoes, North Cheyennes, and the different bands of the Sioux. Their depredations had extended east to the Missouri River, and General Pope sent General Sully with a force up that river to take care of the hostile Sioux that had gathered and had been fighting the troops at Forts Rice, Berthoud, and other points. Before reaching these posts his column was turned and sent to Devil's Lake after the Santee Sioux, who had been committing depredations in Minnesota, but after reaching the lake he failed to find any Indians, they having fled to the British Possessions. He returned to the Missouri River and endeavored to make terms with the tribes concentrated on it, but only partially succeeded. We knew that there were from two to three thousand of the Sioux, Cheyennes and Arapahoes concentrated at or near Bear Butte, near the north end of the Black Hills, and it was the intention of General Sully with his force to go after this band, but, being turned to the east, I organized a force about 1,000 strong under Colonel Nelson Cole, who went up the Missouri River in boats to Omaha and whose orders were to move from Omaha to Columbus up the Loup Fork to its head and thence across the Niobrara to the White Earth River and then to Bear Butte. Failing to find the Indians there, he was to push on to Powder and Tongue Rivers, where he was to join Brigadier-General P. E. Connor, who was in command of this district. Lieutenant-Colonel Samuel Walker's column of about 500 men of the Sixteenth Kansas Cavalry was to go north from Fort Laramie along the west base of the Black Hills and join Colonel Cole, and later join General Connor on the Tongue River; while General Connor, with a small command of about 500 men, [Pg 86] was moving north along the Platte to the head of Salt Creek down the Salt to Powder River, where he was to establish a fort and supply station; from thence he was to move along the east base of the Big Horn Mountains until he struck the hostile Indians in that vicinity. These columns should have moved in May or June, but it was July and August before they got started, on account of the failure of the contractors to deliver the supplies to them on the plains at the different supply-depots; but when they started they moved with alacrity, and would, no doubt, have accomplished the purpose of the campaign had it not been for the fact that they were stopped by an order from Washington to return to Fort Laramie by October 15th.

During May, June, and July the Indians were very aggressive all along the South Platte and North Platte routes. Every Government train had to go guarded; every emigrant train had to be organized into trains of 50 or 100 wagons, with the teamsters armed and placed under an officer, and even then a great many of their people were killed and a great deal of stock run off. The commanding officer at Fort Laramie, during June, had concentrated at his post about 2,000 of what was considered friendly Indians. Most of these Indians had been captured during the spring campaign. They had brought in with them most of the prisoners that had been captured on their raids upon the stage-lines and the ranches. General Connor, desiring to get these Indians removed as far as possible from the hostile Indians, under my order moved them south toward the Republican River, in charge of two companies of the Seventh Iowa Cavalry, commanded by Captain Fouts. These Indians did not take kindly to this movement, and the escort sent with them was not as large as it ought to have been. When they were sixty miles south of Fort Laramie they were communicated with by a band of hostile Indians who followed down the opposite side of the Platte River, and early in the morning they attacked their escort, killing Captain Fouts and four soldiers, and wounding seven others. In the fight there were a great many Indians killed and wounded, but these Indians were allowed to go south with their arms, to convince them that we put confidence in them and did not treat them as prisoners. With the aid of the other Indians on the north side of the Platte, they forced the escort to intrench itself, by doing which the train and the women and others who had been rescued from the Sioux Indians were saved, as word was [Pg 87] gotten to Fort Laramie and relief was sent. The Indians after this fight crossed the North Platte River and moved north toward the Black Hills.

Colonel Moonlight, in command of Fort Laramie, as soon as he heard of this revolt, went to relieve the intrenched party. The Indians, however, had crossed the Platte River. He followed them. When within ten or fifteen miles of the band, through carelessness in taking care of his horses, the Indians turned upon him, stampeded his stock, and, in fact, drove off 200 or 300 head of it, leaving his command on foot. The attack of the hostiles frightened the horses so that they could not be controlled, and they ran towards the Indians. Moonlight and his command had to march back to Laramie, a long distance, without food or transportation, as they had started out with only one or two days' rations. Colonel Moonlight was immediately relieved of his command, but the damage had been done, which gave the hostile Indians great encouragement. General Connor sent this dispatch:

Julesburg, June 15, 1865.
(Received 9:50 p. m.)

Major-General Dodge:

I ordered the Indians who surrendered at Laramie to be sent to Kearney. Colonel Moonlight sent them without first dismounting them, under charge of two companies of Seventh Iowa Cavalry.

They revolted sixty miles this side of Laramie, killing Captain Fouts, who was in command, and four soldiers, and wounding seven; also killed four of their own chiefs who refused to join them; fifteen Indians were killed; the Indians fled north with their ponies, women, and children, leaving all their camp equipage. Troops are in pursuit. Mail-stages have stopped west of Camp Collins. Everything appears to work unfavorably owing to failure of corn contractors and incompetency of some of my subordinates. I will overcome all obstacles, however, in a short time. Have you sent me cavalry yet? J. D. Doty, Governor of Utah, was buried at Camp Douglas Cemetery this morning. Died of heart disease.

P. E. Connor,
Brigadier-General.

During July, a band of the Arapahoes raided the South Platte River stage-line between Fort Collins and Fort Halleck, drove off most of the stock from the stations, and committed other depredations. Colonel Porter, who was in command of that district, concentrated his force and went after the Indians, and in a very few days restored the stage stations and gave the Indians sound whippings, which kept that line clear nearly all summer. The Indians that had done this work had gone into Fort Collins claiming to be friendly and wishing to make a treaty, and after being fed there for some time, left one night and committed the depredations before troops could stop them. From here they moved immediately [Pg 88] north to join the hostile Indians north of the North Platte. I had received notice from Washington that the Interior Department had information that these Indians were peaceable and would not join in the campaigns; but, being on the ground, I knew better, because we were capturing them in nearly all of the attacks that they made. With them was a portion of one of the bands of the Sioux.

On July 27, ten miles west of the North Platte Bridge station, a Mormon train coming east was attacked by the Indians and Lieutenant Casper W. Collins, of the Eleventh Ohio, and twenty-five men of the Eleventh Kansas, went out to relieve it, when about one thousand Indians attacked him. While he saved the train he lost his own life, and twenty-five of his men were scalped and their bodies horribly mutilated; but while the Indians had heavy losses in the fight, they were able to divide up and scatter before any of the troops sent to attack them could reach them. I named the post at Platte Bridge Fort Casper, and it is now known as the town of Casper, on the North-Western railroad.

On August 16th a large band of Sioux Indians attacked a military station on the South Platte route. They were overtaken by the Pawnee Indian Battalion of our forces, who gave them a good whipping. They killed a large number and took their stock and scattered them. This was a band of Sioux Indians that had been lying on the North Platte and made this dash to the South Platte stage-line, thinking we had withdrawn the troops from it to the northern expedition. Very few of them ever got back to their tribes.

The battalion of Pawnees with General Conner had made a great capture of a band of Cheyennes who had been down on the Fort Halleck route. The latter had there captured a part of a company of a Michigan Regiment who were escorting a few wagons, the captives having been tied to the wagons and burned. By some means, General Conner got word of this, and knew the trail they would take to get back to the main command, and on this trail he placed Major North and his battalion of Pawnees. Major North, in describing to me what followed, said that when the Indians came back and discovered that they were surrounded, one, an old man, moved up towards him and placed his hand up to his mouth, telling him to come on; that they were ready to die; that they were full of white men up to that,—meaning up to his mouth. [Pg 89] The Pawnees killed every one of this band and scalped them. On one of them was found a diary of one of the Michigan soldiers who had been killed, and one of the Cheyennes had used the book to give an account of their travels, their camps and fights, and what they had done on this raid. From this diary our guides could tell just exactly where the party had been, where they had camped, where they had captured the Michigan soldiers, and their route on their return. A half-breed had written in the book a defiance of the troops, telling what the Indians demanded. Among other things they demanded that before they would make peace we should give up all their prisoners; that we should abandon the country north of the Platte River, etc.

As soon as General Connor reached Powder River he established his post and named it Fort Connor. (It was afterward named Fort Reno by me.) Connor immediately pushed on to the Crazy Woman Mountain fork of Powder River and then to the east base of the Big Horn Mountains, following that to the Tongue River and down the Tongue until James Bridger, the chief scout and guide of the expedition, claimed to have seen the smoke a long distance away, of an Indian camp. No one else could see it, but, as a precaution, Connor sent out the Pawnee scouts, and on August 27th they discovered about 2,000 Indians camped on the Tongue River, near the mouth of Wolf Creek. It is a singular fact that in this vicinity General Crook fought his great battle on the Rosebud, the Custer massacre occurred, and it was not very far away that the Phil Kearney disaster occurred, when Lieutenant Fetterman and his whole command was slaughtered. General Connor immediately corralled the trains and took his available forces, about 250 men, and marched all night and struck this band at daylight, giving them a complete surprise. They were Arapahoes under Black Bear and Old David, with several other noted chiefs. The band was just breaking up their camp, but the Indian soldiers rallied and fought desperately. Captain H. E. Palmer, A. A. G., with General Connor, gives this description of the attack:

The word was passed back for the men to close up and follow the General and not to fire a shot until he fired in advance. General Conner then took the lead, riding his horse up the steep bank of the ravine and dashing out across the mesa as if there were no Indians just to his left. Every man followed as close as possible. At the first sight of the General the Indian ponies grazing on the table-land in front of us sent up a tremendous whinnying, and galloped down toward the Indian village. More [Pg 90] than 1,000 dogs began to bark, and more than 700 Indians made the air ring with their fearful yelling. It appeared that the Indians were in the act of breaking camp. The most of their tepees were down and packed for the march. The ponies, more than 3,000, had been gathered in and most of the squaws and children were mounted, some of them having taken the line of march up the stream to the new camp. The General watched the movements of his men until he saw the last man emerge from the ravine, when he wheeled on the left into line. The whole line then fired a volley into the village without stopping their horses, and the bugles sounded a charge. Not a man but realized that the charge into the village without a moment's hesitation was our only salvation. We already saw that we were greatly outnumbered, and that only desperate fighting would save our scalps. We were in the village in the midst of a hand-to-hand fight with the warriors and squaws, for many of the squaws did as brave fighting as their savage lords. Unfortunately for the squaws and children, our men had no time to direct their aim, and bullets from both sides and murderous arrows filled the air. Women and children fell among the killed and wounded. The scene was indescribable. Each man seemed an army by himself. Near the sweathouse I emptied my revolver into the carcasses of three warriors. One of our men, a member of the Eleventh Ohio Cavalry, a fine-looking soldier with as handsome a face as I ever saw on a man, grabbed me by the shoulder and turned me about that I might assist him in drawing an arrow from his mouth. Having no surgeon of a higher grade than a hospital steward, it was decided that in order to get the arrow out of his mouth the tongue would have to be cut out, which was done. The Indians made a brave stand trying to save their families, and succeeded in getting away with a large majority of their women and children, leaving behind nearly all of their plunder.

We now went up a stream called Wolf Creek, General Connor in close pursuit. Soon after we left the village General Connor advised me to instruct Captain North to take his battalion of Indians and get all the stock he could possibly gather. General Connor pursued the savages fully ten miles from camp, when he found himself accompanied by only fourteen men. Our horses were so worn out that it was impossible for the men to keep up. The Indians noticed his movements and turned upon him and his soldiers. They fell back as fast as possible. Captain North and myself had succeeded in coralling about a thousand ponies. Scores of buffalo-robes, blankets, and furs were heaped up on lodge-poles, and on these we placed our dead, and burned their bodies to keep the Indians from mutilating them. Our attack on the village began at 9 a. m. We remained until 2:30 and had destroyed a great deal of Indian property. At 2:30 we took up the line of march for the corralled train. Captain North with his eighty Indians undertook to drive the captured stock. They were soon a great ways ahead, while the rest of the force was engaged in beating back the Indians. The Indians pressed on every side. They seemed to have plenty of ammunition, but they did most of their fighting with arrows. Before dark we were reduced to forty men, and had only a little ammunition. The Indians showed no signs of stopping the fight, but kept on charging on us, dashing away at the stock, and keeping us constantly on the move until fifteen minutes of twelve, when the last shot was fired by our pursuers. The incidents of this fight would make very interesting reading. Every man was a general. Not a man in the company but realized that his life was in the balance. We must either whip the Indians and whip them badly or be whipped ourselves. We could see that the Indians greatly outnumbered us, but we were better armed than they. As for fighting qualities the savages proved themselves as brave as any of our men. We had accomplished a great deal; 250 Indian lodges and their contents had been burned, with the entire winter's supplies; the son of Black Bear was killed: sixty-three Indians were killed, 1,100 ponies were captured, and a lot of women and children were taken prisoners.

[Pg 91] General Connor's report of this battle was burned in Utah, and consequently was never forwarded to me or to the Government, so we do not know what the loss on his part was; but it was severe.

General Connor now moved down the Tongue River to make a connection with Colonel Walker and Colonel Cole, at the appointed rendezvous. His scouts discovered that Colonel Cole in moving north had endeavored to reach the mouth of Powder River and had failed, and after six days' fighting had marched south, expecting to go to Port Laramie, not knowing that there were supplies at Fort Connor.

Colonel Cole, who with his column had started from Omaha, had made reasonable progress, following out the routes laid down, and did not discover any Indians until he reached the Little Missouri River, on a branch of the Piney that he was coming down. Lieutenant-Colonel Walker, of the center column, visited his camp and was two days behind him. He should have immediately joined him, to carry out his instructions. Cole was headed toward the Tongue

River, near the Wolf Mountains. When he got into the brakes of the Powder River, he discovered many signs of Indians. This is a very rough country, and he had great difficulty in getting his long trains through it; however, he dropped into the valley about fifty miles above the mouth of Powder River and sent a detachment with his best guide fifty miles across to Tongue River and Panther Mountains and discovered nothing of Connor. In Cole's instructions he was told that there would be a supply-depot at Panther or Wolf Mountains, but General Connor had changed this and made the supply-depot at what was known as Camp Connor, on Powder River, and he did not notify either Cole or Walker of this change, which he should have done, as had he done so it would have avoided all the trouble that these two columns encountered. Cole's detachment of cavalry discovered no signs of Connor on Tongue River and so followed down the river, while they should have gone up; and failing to find any sign of any depot at Panther Mountains, reported back to Cole. Cole's rations were now exhausted, or nearly so, as he had not been as careful of them as he should have been, expecting as he did to find a depot where he could get plenty at the end of his sixty days' march. It shows that he was not up to the woodcraft of the country. In examining Powder River towards its mouth he found it destitute of grass and full of canyons. He, therefore, made up his mind to move south up the Powder [Pg 92] River valley, with a view to either meeting Connor or making for Fort Laramie. The Indians, seeing this retreat, became very bold. There were at least 2,000 of them, Cheyennes and Sioux, and without making an attack they simply harassed him, sometimes forcing a fight; but very few were hurt. Colonel Cole should have parked his train, placed it in a defensive position under a good guard, and then mobilized the rest of his force, and, with what rations he had, gone after the Indians, giving them battle and forcing the fight with them. He had plenty of men.

Cole had not advanced very far towards Port Connor when, on September 6th, Colonel Walker and his command joined him. Then he had plenty of men to meet all the Indians in the country, if his force was properly handled. When this fighting commenced he was not over thirty miles from where Connor fought his battle, and Captain Palmer states that they heard a cannon, but could not tell which direction the noise came from. Connor, hearing nothing from Cole, sent out Major North with a couple of Indian scouts and with Bridger as guide. They got over into the Powder River country and discovered Cole's trail. During Cole's retreat up the Powder there came a fearful snow-storm. The animals having marched so far without grain, were already very much exhausted, and the storm lasting three days, they became so weak that they were not fit to use, and they were therefore shot, just as they stood at the picket-line, to prevent them from falling into the Indians' hands. This destruction of the animals and the burning of all their equipment was about the first thing that Major North struck, and of course he experienced a great anxiety, fearing that Cole had met with great disaster, and immediately reported to General Connor, who at once sent Sergeant C. L. Thomas with two Pawnees with dispatches to Colonel Cole to march on up Powder River to Fort Connor, where he would find supplies. Cole's troops seem to have started out not fully prepared for such a trip, especially in the line of shoes and leggings, although they were carefully instructed by me to be sure to take a surplus, as I knew the country. Cole's excuse is that while he made ample requisition, the Quartermaster never shipped them, and so when he reached Omaha he had to buy such as he could find. Colonel Cole's troops seem to have kept up their organization and their fighting qualities, for whenever they met the Indians they always whipped them; but they were on the retreat, which gave every advantage to the Indians. When [Pg 93] Cole's troops reached Port Connor they were in a deplorable condition—ragged, barefooted, and almost without rations and ammunition.

The Indians surrounding Fort Connor at this time had become so numerous that the commanding officer thought it prudent to intrench the post, which shows good judgment; but Colonel Cole complains in his report that the troops were made to help do this intrenching. Speaking of this he says:

While camped here (Fort Connor) an occurrence took place, strange but most true, which as an integral part of the closing history of the command must have full relation. Some thirty-six hours after reaching this post, a fatigued detail of 400 men was ordered from the Second Missouri Light Artillery to work on the earthworks being thrown up around the place. If the spirit that prompted the detail expected to force its principles through insubordination or rebellion, it was disappointed. What a sight was here! Four hundred ragged, bare-footed men, emaciated with fatigue, who had met and worsted the enemy on three several occasions, marched up in the face of a garrison of 2,000 or more.

I don't know where he got the 2,000 troops, as all the troops when he reached Fort Connor were two companies of Michigan cavalry, General Connor then not having reached that post; and when he did, all told there were not 2,000 troops there. Cole's loss was very light, — nine killed, — while he claims to have killed from 200 to 500 of the Indians.

It was very evident to me that there was no very severe fighting here; it was simply a skirmish on a retreat.

Lieutenant-Colonel Walker's column, which started from Fort Laramie on August 2d, moved up the west base of the Black Hills, and struck Cole's column on August 20th on what was known as Piney Creek. After striking Cole's trail he followed it a short distance, and then left it and struck Powder River, much farther south than Cole had, and on reaching the river he fell right into the same band of Indians that were gathered along the Powder River to harass Cole. He, too, was short of provisions, although he was equipped to travel very rapidly, having all his supplies on pack-mules. As soon as he got in touch with Cole he joined him and followed him to Fort Connor. General Connor's idea was to make up a rapid-moving column of about 1,000 men, using the pack-mules of Walker, and then combine his and Cole's troops to move on a line farther to the west and follow these Indians to the British Possessions if necessary. He had the ammunition, equipment and everything at Fort Connor to fit out these columns with. As near as they could estimate there were about 6,000 Indians all told.

[Pg 94]

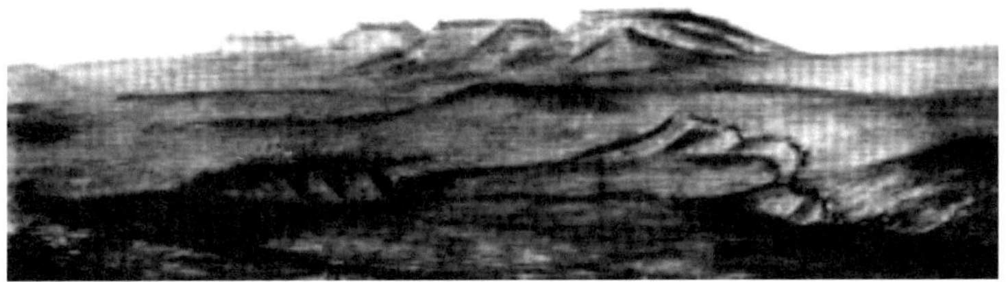

PUMPKIN BUTTES

Prominent land-mark near where Colonels Cole and Walker fought the Indians in September, 1865, on Powder River.

[Pg 95] The wagon-road train that started from Sioux City under Colonel Sawyer's engineering party, with two companies of the Fifth United States Volunteer Infantry under the command of Captain George N. Williford, that were to open a wagon-road from Sioux City up the Niobrara River by a short route to the north end of the Black Hills, intended to cross to Powder River and then to the south end of the Big Horn Mountains, making a direct emigrant route into Montana. As soon as I heard of the instructions given this expedition I got word to Colonel Sawyer that it was impossible for him to travel on that route; that he must keep to the south end of the Black Hills and follow up the North Platte until he struck what was known as the Bozeman trail, that was laid out in 1864 by some emigrants going into Montana. This was the trail that Connor had taken on his route to Tongue River. It was feasible all the way from the Platte to Montana. Colonel Sawyer paid no attention to this information, but kept on his original route until he got into the brakes of the Powder River, not very far from where Cole struck them. When within twenty miles of the River, he ascertained by his own guide that it was impossible to advance any farther in that direction; consequently, he had to retrace his steps. On the second day they were attacked by a large band of Indians; evidently the Cheyennes and Sioux that afterwards attacked Colonels Cole and Walker. These Indians kept them corralled nearly four days and nights, fighting through the day and withdrawing at night, only to begin their hostilities at dawn; but finding that their efforts only resulted in many being killed, they abandoned the siege and left, going south, striking Cole's trail on August 22d, which they followed, and on the 23d Colonel Sawyer marched into Port Connor. While Captain Williford does not say that he took charge of this train, that is a fact. He took charge of it and kept it until he got to Fort Connor. He was a splendid officer and it was through his good judgment and his ability as a soldier that he saved the whole outfit. The Bent Boys, who were at the head of the Cheyennes, would communicate with Sawyer and get him to send out persons for the purpose of trading with them, and whoever was sent inside their lines was held prisoner, the idea being to wear Sawyer's force out by this means. But they struck the wrong man in Captain Williford, who, comprehending the [Pg 96] situation, attacked the Indians. I knew Williford in the Civil War, and he was a very efficient officer. At Fort Connor I relieved Williford, his men being mostly barefooted, and put Colonel Kidd of the Michigan Cavalry, in command, with a suitable escort, and instructed him to follow the Connor trail until they struck Tongue River, and then to swing towards the Yellowstone and strike the trail up that river to Bozeman. This train, when they got nearly opposite to where General Connor fought, was again attacked by the Indians; but Colonel Kidd managed to get news to General Connor and he sent two or three companies of his command to the rescue. They were absent while he fought his battle on Tongue River. They drove off the Indians, and relieved the train, which reached Montana in safety.

Early in September I reached Fort Connor—before General Cole and Colonel Walker had concentrated there—and gave instructions under the direction of the authorities at Washington, forwarded to me by General Pope, to withdraw all the troops to Fort Laramie, and stop all their operations against the Indians, and endeavor to bring them in for a consultation, and, if possible, to make an agreement as to the cessation of all hostilities. This was a fatal mistake. When I received this dispatch from General Pope, on August 31st, I sent the following message to him:

Headquarters U. S. Forces.
Fort Laramie, Dakota Territory, August 31, 1865.

Major-General John Pope, St. Louis, Mo.:

I consider the Indian matters here of so much importance, and knowing no one can judge of them so well as when he is on the ground, that I desire to make a proposition to the Government. If the Government will allow me to keep General Connor in the field with not to exceed 2,000 men of his present force, leaving the forces you have designated to garrison posts on the plains. I will settle these Indian difficulties before spring satisfactorily to the Government, and bring about a peace that will be lasting. I may do it in a month or two; or it may be longer. The additional expense to the Government will be the pay of that number of troops for the time detained. All the stores, forage, etc., to support them are here and *en route.* As soon as we settle with them we can send these troops in and take 2,000 more from our posts in addition and muster them out. General Connor left Powder River with sixty days' supplies, and I am satisfied if we will allow him he will settle the matter before he returns. Should he come back by our orders without settling the matter, the entire Indian tribes will be down on our lines, and we will have our hands full, and more too. The forces for Utah I will soon have on the road, and when Connor gets back he can go right there.

G. M. Dodge,
Major-General.

General Connor, after getting news of the position of Cole's and Walker's forces, moved back with his forces to Fort Connor, [Pg 97] with a view of taking command of Cole's and Walker's forces and organizing them into two columns—one a light column with pack-mules, and the other with the trains,—and then to follow and attack the Indians that had been fighting Cole and Walker. When he arrived at Fort Connor he found my dispatches, which, of course, changed his whole policy. He knew then where all the Indians were located. They had all been forced away from the traveled lines to protect their villages, and it was only a question of time—weeks or months—before we would have conquered a peace that the Indians would have recognized.

The dispatches which I sent from Fort Laramie brought an answer from General Grant to the effect that the authorities at Washington were determined to stop all campaigns against the Indians. They had been made to believe by the Interior Department that all they had to do was to withdraw the troops and the Indians would come in and make peace. On my return from Fort Connor, when I reached the North Platte I sent this dispatch:

Horseshoe, September 15, 1865.

Major-General John Pope, St. Louis:

Arrived here today on my return from Powder River. That post is well located, right in heart of Indian country, and is an important post. The Indians' trails all cross at or near it, and it will have good effect hereafter in holding in check Indians. Have not heard from General Connor since August 24. We cannot reach him now. They have done a good deal of work on Powder River; got up stockade and commenced Quartermaster buildings; well under way. Great lack of Quartermaster's stores up there, the Powder River stores not having reached Laramie yet. From Laramie to Powder River, then to Virginia City, is an excellent wagon-road; good grass, water, and wood all the way, and the most direct road that can be got. The travel over it in another season will be immense; it saves at least 450 miles in distance. After the Indians attacked Colonel Sawyer's wagon-road party and failed in their attempt, they held a parley. Colonel Bent's sons, George and Charles Bent, appeared on part of Indians, and Colonel Sawyer gave them a wagon-load of goods to let him go undisturbed, Captain Williford, commanding escort, not agreeing to it. The Indians accepted proposition and agreed to it, but after receiving the goods they attacked party; killed three men. Bent said that there was one condition on which the Cheyennes would treat; viz., the hanging by Government of Colonel Chivington. He also said that the Indians considered that they were strong enough to fight the Government; preferred to do it; that they knew the Government would withdraw troops in fall; then they would have it all their own way again. Expressed great fear about Connor, and said they were concentrating everything to meet him, which is true. Since he left no Indians have troubled the mail- or telegraph-lines, but are all moving north, stragglers and all. At Fort Connor they kill a few of them as they pass every few days. There is one band of Arapahoes in Medicine Bow Mountains, who are committing depredations around Denver, on Cache La Poudre and Big Thompson Creeks. They belong to the band that was at Cow Creek treaty. I shall be in Laramie tomorrow; see General Wheaton; thence to Denver. Bent also said that some of tribes had agreed to make peace on Missouri River, but they were doing this to keep us from [Pg 98] sending a force that way. These Bent boys were educated in St. Louis. One has been with Price in the rebel Army; was captured. His father got him released and took him to his ranch on the Arkansas River, when he joined the Cheyennes, of which he is a halfbreed. He was dressed in one of our staff officer's uniforms.

G. M. Dodge,
Major-General.

On General Connor's arrival at Fort Connor he wired me the results of the campaign and protested strenuously against the order stopping it, saying he was then in condition and position to close it, conquer the Indians, and force a lasting peace. On receipt of his report I sent this dispatch:

Central City, Colo., September 27, 1865.

Major-General John Pope, St. Louis, Mo.:

On August 28th, General Connor surprised Medicine Man's band of Indians on Tongue River; killed fifty; captured village, all winter provisions, and 600 horses—all the stock they had. On the 1st of September the right column, under Colonel Cole, had a fight with the Sioux, Cheyennes, and Arapahoes, on Powder River, and whipped them. On the evening of the 3d of September attacked them again, driving them down Powder River ten miles. Next morning at daylight attacked again, fight lasting until 10 a. m., when Indians were defeated with loss of 200 killed. They fled in every direction, losing large number of horses, camp equipage, provisions, etc. On 8th instant, Colonel Walker, commanding center column, who was in advance of Colonel Cole, met Indians in large force. Colonel Cole came up and after a short but spirited engagement they totally routed Indians, driving them in every direction with great loss, several of principal chiefs being killed in this fight. On the night of the 9th of September a severe snow-storm raged, in which 400 of Colonel Cole's horses perished. I was in that storm on Powder River. It was very severe, and I lost several animals. Our total loss in all the engagements not more than fifty killed and wounded, including one officer. Colonel Cole or Colonel Walker had not communicated with General Connor and were on Powder River, but by this time they have communicated, as they had ascertained where General Connor's column was.

G. M. Dodge,
Major-General.

General Connor, in compliance with his orders, moved south from Fort Connor to distribute at the different posts where they had been assigned, the forces not ordered to be mustered out. As soon as he started south to Fort Laramie the Indians followed him and swarmed immediately on the overland routes, both the North and South Platte, reaching even as far as the Arkansas, and committed great depredations. The troops along those lines had been mustered out, and the regular-army force that was to take their places had not arrived. It was a harvest for the Indians. In my absence General Pope had assigned to the different districts regular-army officers for permanent command. They were to take the places of the volunteers. Under my instructions I immediately sent word to the Indians to come to Fort Laramie for the purpose of a [Pg 99] consultation. To accomplish this I sent out the best-posted guides (using chiefs, sub-chiefs, half-breeds of friendly Indians) that I knew on the plains, to each of the hostile tribes asking them to come into Fort Laramie. I instructed the messengers to tell them that if any of their people had gone to the Missouri River for peaceable purposes to let them go, but to bring in all that were left, providing they felt disposed to settle without delay. I sent them word that if they did not come in and settle they would find that our summer campaign was only a taste of what they would get this winter, for we would give them no rest. I posted the district commanders thoroughly, telling them what we wanted was to settle with the Indians before they discovered the smallness of our forces on the plains. I told them they might say, also, that all of the Indians south of the Arkansas had made peace, and gave instructions that they be told about the battle with the Arapahoes and Cheyennes on Powder and Tongue Rivers. I sent the district commanders word to show Big Ribs, one of my messengers, the forces at their posts, and to impress upon him our power. The effect of this appeal to the different tribes was that early in the spring of 1866 we got together at Fort Laramie the principal chiefs and the head men of the North Cheyennes, Arapahoes, and the different tribes of the Sioux, when a council was held.

I had instructed General Frank Wheaton, who commanded at Fort Laramie, that we would agree to almost anything to bring a permanent peace except to allow the Indians to come down to the North Platte and occupy the country through which the new military road was laid out to Bozeman, Mont. Our troops, in passing up the east base of the Black Hills, had discovered gold. There were Colorado and California Regiments in the commands, and I knew, and so did General Connor, that many were preparing, as soon as a treaty was made, to go back into that country and prospect it, and I gave that reason to the Indians for holding them north of the Belle Fourche Fork of the Cheyenne River; but that country was their best hunting-ground. They were perfectly willing to give up all the country south of the Platte River, and not to interfere with the building of the Union Pacific road or with any of the overland routes up the North or South Platte; but they would not consent to give up the Black Hills north of the North Platte. Finally we made an agreement with them that they should occupy the country north of the North Platte River until such time [Pg 100] as the Government should see proper to send a commission out to negotiate a permanent peace with them. I gave instructions to tell them that if the white men went into their territory and we did not keep them out, they were at liberty to do so. I knew that would deter any white man going in there, and as long as they kept the peace, we would. Red Cloud, who had then come to the head of the Ogalalla band of the Sioux Indians, took a prominent part in this conference, and was backed by such chiefs as Spotted Tail, Man-Afraid-of-His-Horses, Big Ribs, and the Bent boys on behalf of the Cheyennes. He declared that they would never give up their country north of the Platte. "You may take my country," said Red Cloud, "but I will mark every mile of that Bozeman trail from the North Platte to Yellowstone with the bodies of your soldiers;" and this he pretty nearly accomplished. This agreement, made at Fort Laramie, accomplished nothing. During the years 1866, 1867 and 1868 the Indians swarmed across the lines agreed upon and occupied the country, especially along the Union Pacific, which was then being constructed through that country. The Government had to send in additional troops, and all the military posts over the country had to be re-occupied the same as they had been before. The Government endeavored to again reach these Indians through a peace commission in 1868. General W. T. Sherman was at the head of it, and it was composed of General Harney and others. They visited me at Fort Sanders, Wyo., before they went to make a treaty with the Indians, and wished to know my reasons for the position I took in the consultation of 1866. I then told General Sherman that my soldiers had found gold in all the streams heading in the Black Hills north of the North Platte, and that as soon as he allowed those Indians to come to the North Platte under a treaty of peace, he would not be across the Missouri River on his return before that country would be covered by prospectors from California and Colorado. General Sherman answered that their instructions were to make such a peace and they were sent there to do it, and, sure enough, they did; and as soon as the treaty was made the miners poured into the country. One of the first mines that was discovered was the Homestake or Homestead. Sitting Bull, who had taken part in this treaty and whose country was the Black Hills, sent in protest after protest, demanding that the Government live up to the terms of the treaty and drive the miners out, but no attention was paid to them. The miners and [Pg 101] settlers poured into the Black Hills country and drove the Indians out, and Sitting Bull said in a conference he had with some of the Army officers in the 70's that if the Government did not protect their territory as provided in the treaty, they would themselves; and they started to do it. The massacres of that year came from his band, the troubles finally ending with the sacrifice of the Custer Regiment in 1876. While this was a horrible event, the Indians, under the treaty, were fully justified in it. During this same time Red Cloud occupied the Bozeman trail. He killed emigrants, besides murdering Captain Fetterman and his company at Fort Phil Kearney, and other troops located at the posts that we established along there in 1866, such as Forts Reno, McKinney, Phil Kearney, and C. F. Smith. It was not until after the Custer massacre that these Indians were brought to time and put on reservations; since then peace has prevailed.

The Government had the same difficulty on the Arkansas River route that we had on the Platte routes in the summer of 1866, 1867, and 1868. The Indians that had made the agreement with Colonel Leavenworth were all committing depredations until finally the Government sent General Sheridan there with instructions to punish them. They tried to play the same game with Sheridan that they had played with us, but he would have none of it. There was no one in Washington who would force him to listen to the appeals of the peace commission. His troops, under Colonels Custer, Evans, and others, fought three battles south of the Arkansas, noticeably wiping out some bands, and making them give up their prisoners, stop their murders, and go on reservations in the Indians' territory. From that time on they have been peaceable.

We were much better prepared, in the fall of 1865, both on the Arkansas and on the Yellowstone, to conquer these Indians. We had got up to their villages and had plenty of troops, plenty of provisions, and plenty of clothing, and could carry on the campaign through the winter, if necessary; and so, if we had allowed General Ford or General Sanborn to have gone forward with the columns and punish those southern Indians, they would have made a permanent peace. But the fact is the Indians did not give up until they were thoroughly thrashed and made to recognize the power and authority of the Government.

[Pg 102] The policy of the United States in dealing with the Indian problem is beyond the comprehension of any sensible man. They were treated the same as foreign nations; and while they made treaties they never carried out their part of them, breaking them whenever the trend of civilization westward interfered with them in any way. The Government attempted to deal with and govern the Indians with civil agents and at the same time tried to enforce peace through the military authorities. This caused friction; and deception and cheating in the supplying of them through their contractors and civil agents brought untold complaints. If the Government had treated the Indians as a ward that they were bound to protect, as the English did, they would have had very little trouble in handling them. The military force would have held all conferences with them; fed them when they needed it; located them in an early day on unoccupied good hunting-grounds; and finally, as civilization moved into their territories and as their tribes wasted away, would have given them reservations where the Government from the money they received from the lands the Indians claimed, could have kept and fed them without any great burden or cost. In all the days of Indian warfare and treaties, there never was such a farce, or failure to comprehend the frontier situation, as in the years 1865 and 1866, and the failure of the Government to take advantage of the comprehensive plans instituted by the military authorities, as well as of the great expenditures made, and to punish the Indians as they deserved, brought, in after years, greater expenditures and more disturbances than ever.

Early in the campaign, after General Pope had made known his views to the Government, he requested me to write fully mine to the Secretary of the Interior, who had charge of Indian affairs, and who was from my state, and I sent him this letter:

Headquarters Department of the Missouri.
St. Louis, Mo., June 22, 1865.

Hon. James Harlan, Secretary of the Interior, Washington, D. C.:

My Dear Sir: Copies of Senator Doolittle's and Commissioner Dole's letters to you of dates May 31 and June 12 have been furnished me. My acquaintance with you leads me to believe that you are endeavoring to get at the real facts of our Indian difficulties and the best methods for putting an end to them. So far as Senator Doolittle's letter refers to "some general getting up of an Indian war on his own hook" and for his own purposes, I shall indulge no reply. You know me, and if it was intended in any way to apply to me I leave you to judge of how much credence should be attached to it. My sincere desire is to terminate these Indian troubles, and I have no hesitation in saying that if I am allowed to carry out the policy [Pg 103] now being pursued toward them I will have peace with them before another emigration crosses the plains. When I assumed command of the former Department of Kansas I found all the important Indian tribes on the plains in open hostility against us. Whether it was the fault of the white man or the Indian, the fact was patent. They were holding the entire overland route from Julesburg to Junction Station, had destroyed the telegraph-lines, captured trains, burned ranches, and murdered men, women, and children indiscriminately. I soon stopped these proceedings, opened our broken lines of communication; repaired, so far as possible, the injury done; pushed troops out there, and then tried to effect a settlement with the Indians. On the southern route I found a similar state of affairs existing. The Indians were on the warpath, and I at once started expeditions against them, learning of which Colonel Leavenworth, Indian Agent, informed me that he could make peace with them; that we were at fault, etc. I stopped my expeditions on the southern route to give him an opportunity to accomplish this object. He started for their camps; they robbed him, stole his mules, and he hardly escaped with his scalp; and on his return stated that it was useless to attempt to make peace with them. I then, in accordance with the orders of the Secretary of War, started for the Indians again, and had just got my forces under way when the committee, of which Senator Doolittle is a member, reached Fort Larned, and after an interview with Colonel Leavenworth, gave orders for the expeditionary movements to stop. The grounds for this action the Senator gives in his letter. I was then aware that the Indians were moving north to attack that line, and was moving two columns in concert with General Ford to intercept and punish them; and I at that time telegraphed that the tribes spoken of by Senator Doolittle were on their way north to attack our trains. They had then driven out all traders, made a treaty with the southern Indians and Texans, and sent me word that they wanted no peace.

Within ten days from the time Senator Doolittle and his party left Fort Larned, and before I had time to countermand their orders and get my troops disposed, the Indians attacked the posts and trains all along the line, running off stock, capturing trains, etc., murdering men, and showing conclusively that they were determined on war at all hazards. Our overtures to them, as well as those of the agents sent out by General Carleton, were treated with disdain. From Fort Laramie I sent word to the Sioux, Cheyennes, etc., that if they wanted peace to come in and stop their hostilities. A few of each tribe responded by coming in; the rest refused, and indicated their purposes and feelings by attacking the posts west of Fort Laramie, and on Laramie Plains, murdering, stealing, etc. I undertook to remove the friendly Indians from Fort Laramie to Fort Kearney, in order to get them away from the troubles. When about sixty miles south of Fort Laramie they attacked their guard, killed a captain and four privates, turned upon five of their chiefs who were disposed to be friendly, killed them, and then escaped, leaving their camps, etc., in our hands; so that now we have every Indian tribe capable of mischief from the British Possessions on the north to the Red River on the south, at war with us, while the whites are backing them up. These facts, it appears to me, are a sufficient answer to the letters of Senator Doolittle and Commissioner Dole. That these Indians have been greatly wronged I have no doubt, and I am certain that the agents who have been connected with them are as much to blame as any one else. So far as the Chivington fight was concerned, it occurred before I assumed command. I condemned it, and I have issued orders that no such acts will be tolerated or allowed; that the Indians on the warpath must be fought wherever and whenever found, but no outrages or barbarities must be committed. I am convinced that the only way to effectually settle these troubles is for us to move our columns directly into their country, punish them when we find them, show them our power, and at the same time give them to know that: we are ready to make [Pg 104] peace with them—not, however, by paying them for murdering our people and plundering our trains and posts, but by informing them that if they will refrain from further hostilities they shall not be molested; that neither agents nor citizens shall be allowed to go among them to swindle them; that we will protect them in their rights; that we will enforce compliance with our part of the treaty, and will require them to do the same on their part. Let them ask for peace. We should keep citizens out of their country. The class of men sent among them as agents go there for no good purpose. They take positions for the sole purpose of making money out of the Indians by swindling them, and so long as they can do this they shield them in their crimes.

Colonel Leavenworth, who stands up so boldly for the southern Indians, was dismissed from the United States service. He "blows hot and cold" with singular grace. To my officers he talks war to the knife; to Senator Doolittle and others he talks peace. Indeed, he is all things to all men. When officers of the army deal with these Indians, if they mistreat them, we have a certain remedy for their cases. They can be dismissed and disgraced, while Indian agents can only be displaced by others perhaps no better. Now I am confident we can settle these Indian difficulties in the manner I have indicated. The

Indians say to me that they will treat with an officer of the army (a brave), in all of whom they seem to have confidence, while they despise and suspect civilian agents and citizens, by whom they say they have been deceived and swindled so much that they put no trust in their words. I have given orders to the commanders of each of my columns that when they have met and whipped these Indians, or even before, if they have an opportunity, to arrange, if possible, an informal treaty with them for a cessation of hostilities, and whatever they agree to do, to live to strictly, allowing no one, either citizen or soldier, to break it. I shall myself go out on the plains in a few weeks and try to get an interview with the chiefs and if possible effect an amicable settlement of affairs; but I am utterly opposed to making any treaty that pays them for the outrages they have committed, or that hires them to keep the peace. Such treaties last just as long as they think them for their benefit, and no longer. As soon as the sugar, coffee, powder, lead, etc., that we give them, is gone, they make war to get us to give them more. We must first punish them until we make them fear us and respect our power, and then we must ourselves live strictly up to the treaties made. No one desires more than I do to effect a permanent peace with these Indians, and such is the desire of every officer under me, all of whom agree in the method suggested for bringing it about.

Very many of these officers on the plains have been there for years, and are well acquainted with these Indians and their character, and my own opinions in this matter are founded not alone from my experience and observations since I have commanded here, but also with intercourse with them on the plains during a number of years prior to the war, in which time I met and had dealings with nearly every tribe east of the Rocky Mountains. Until hostilities cease I trust that you will keep all agents, citizens and traders away from them. When peace is made with them, if civilian agents and citizens are sent among them, send those who you know to be of undoubted integrity. I know you desire to do so, and from the appointments you have already made I believe you will be successful. My plan, however, would be to keep these Indians under the care of officers of the army, stationed in their country; that what is given them be given by these officers, and that all citizens, agents and traders should, while among them, be subject to their (the officers') supervision and police regulations. In this way I have no doubt these Indians can be kept in their own country, their outrages stopped, and our overland routes kept safe. Now, not a train or coach of any kind can cross the plains in safety without being guarded, and I have over 3,000 miles of route to protect and guard. The [Pg 105] statement that the Sand Creek affair was the first Indian aggression is a mistake. For months prior to that affair the Indians had been attacking our trains, posts, and ranches; had robbed the emigrants and murdered any party they considered too weak to defend themselves.

The theory that we cannot punish these Indians effectually, and that we must make or accept any kind of a peace in order to hold our overland routes, is not sustained by the facts, is singularly erroneous, and I cannot agree to it by any means. I have now seven different columns of troops penetrating their country in all directions, while at the same time I am holding the overland routes. This display of force alone will alarm and terrify them; will show them that we are in earnest, have the power, and intend at all hazards to make them behave themselves. After we have taught them this they will sue for peace; then if the government sees fit to indemnify them for any wrongs inflicted upon them, they will not charge it to our fears or inability to cope with them. The cost of carrying on this war with them is, to be sure, considerable; but the question arises, Had we not better bear this cost now while the preparations are made and the force on hand ready to be thrown in such strength into their country as to make quick, effective, and final work of it, than to suffer a continuance of their outrages for a long time and finally have to do the work at greater expense of blood and treasure? I have written you this frankly and truly, knowing that you want to get at the facts and do that which is for the best, and I am convinced that when you fully understand these matters you will agree with me. I shall be glad at any and all times to furnish you any information in my possession that you may desire, and I assure you I shall bend all my energies to the accomplishment of the great object in view and so much desired — a lasting and just peace with these Indians.

I have the honor to be, very respectfully, your obedient servant.

G. M. Dodge,
Major-General Commanding.

Since writing this report of the Indian campaign of 1865 and 1866, I have seen Secretary of the Navy Gideon Wells's diary of the reconstruction period, from which the following extracts are taken:

Tuesday, August 8, 1865.

Stanton submitted a number of not material questions, yet possessed of some little interest. Before the meeting closed the subject of army movements on the plains came up, and Stanton said there were three columns of twenty-two thousand troops moving into the Indian country, with a view to an Indian campaign. Inquiry as to the origin and authority of such a movement elicited nothing from the War Secretary. He said he knew nothing on the subject. He had been told there was such a movement, and Meigs had informed him it was true. Grant had been written to for information, but Grant was away and he knew not when he should have a reply. The expenses of this movement could not, he said, be less than $50,000,000. But he knew nothing about it.

Friday, August 11, 1865.

The question of the Indian war on the plains was again brought forward. No one, it appears, has any knowledge on the question. The Secretary of War is in absolute ignorance. Says he has telegraphed to General Grant, and General Grant says he has not ordered it. McCulloch wanted to know the probable expense—the numbers engaged, etc. Stanton thought McCulloch had better state how many should be engaged—said General Pope had command. Harlan said he considered Pope an improper man—was extravagant and wasteful. Thought twenty-two hundred instead of twenty-two thousand men was a better and sufficient number.

This whole thing is a discredit to the War Department.

[Pg 106] Tuesday, August 15, 1865.

Stanton says there is to be a large reduction of the force which is moving against the Indians. That by the 1st of October the force will be about 6,000. That large supplies have gone on, but they can be divided or deflected to New Mexico and other points, so that they will not be lost.

Friday, August 18, 1865.

Senator Doolittle and Mr. Ford, who have been on a mission to the plains, visiting New Mexico, Colorado, etc., had an interview with the President and Cabinet of an hour and a half. Their statement in relation to the Indians and Indian affairs exhibits the folly and wickedness of the expedition which has been gotten up by somebody without authority or the knowledge of the Government.

Their strong protestations against an Indian war, and their statement of the means which they had taken to prevent it, came in very opportunely. Stanton said General Grant had already written to restrict operations; he had also sent to General Meigs. I have no doubt a check has been put on a very extraordinary and unaccountable proceeding, but I doubt if an active stop is yet put to war expenses.

It is no wonder that with such ignorance in the Cabinet as to the condition of the country, that the administration at Washington was so incompetent in the Civil War. No person can read Secretary Wells's diary of the daily doings at Washington of the Cabinet during President Lincoln's administration and see how little appreciation and support he got from his Cabinet. Dissensions among themselves and hardly ever agreeing on any important question, brings to view the great responsibility of the President and the fact that in all the important matters he was dependent upon his own judgment. The Cabinet knew nothing of the Indian depredations that for three months held all the lines of travel, mail, and telegraph crossing the plains to California, with every State and Territory west of the Missouri River appealing for protection, until President Lincoln wrote to General Grant to try and have something done to protect that country. General Grant instructed me to make the campaign in the winter of 1864-65, which was so successful that in forty days all the overland routes were opened, and the stage, telegraph, and mails replaced, as shown in my reports, though at the beginning of the campaign every tribe of Indians from the British Possessions to the Indian Territory was at war, with captures and murders of settlers along all the overland routes, in all the frontier States, every-day occurrences; with women and children captured and outrages committed that cannot be mentioned. And yet this Cabinet had no knowledge of the conditions, and concluded from the report of the Doolittle Peace Commission that the Indian expedition was a complete failure, notwithstanding that this commission failed to make ponce with a single tribe of [Pg 107] Indians and failed to stop the depredations of any band of Indians; and, upon its report, declaring that the Indian expeditions were a folly and wickedness gotten up by some one without the authority or knowledge of the Government.

There never were 22,000 troops on the plains, nor one-half of that number. The War Department may have sent that number out, but, as I have shown, they were all mustered out before they reached their work; and the cost of the campaign with a year's supplies at the posts for all the troops on the plains or engaged in the campaign was not more than $10,000,000, a very small amount compared with the trouble and cost of fighting these Indians for ten years thereafter. Secretary Harlan says that 2,200 troops were sufficient. When I took command, in January, 1865, there were not to exceed 5,000 troops guarding trains, stages, and telegraph-lines, and protecting all the routes of travel across the plains, and they had utterly failed. All travel had been stopped and no expeditions against the Indians had been made. The Indians had held the overland routes for three months in spite of these troops. It shows how little knowledge Secretary Harlan had of the condition of Indian affairs in his department. From the statements of Secretary Wells it is evident where the order came from to stop all operations on the plains and withdraw all troops by October 15th. When Secretary Stanton states that by October 1st the troops on the plains would be reduced to 6,000, it shows how little knowledge he had of affairs in his department, for at that time there were not 6,000 troops on the plains or in my command.

It is well that no one knew the condition of affairs; that no one was aware of the ignorance of the group of statesmen at Washington who were supposed to be responsible for our nation and its preservation. They did not seem to know where to ascertain the facts. It would seem that Secretary Stanton purposely wished to place a reflection on General Grant, for he must have known that he was responsible for the Army and for all of its movements. It seems that General Grant was away at the time the dispatches of General Pope and myself were sent showing the necessity of continuing the campaign and punishing these savages. When he returned he tried to stop this Cabinet panic, but his dispatches in answer to those from Pope and myself show that he could not do it, and the fatal mistake was made of stopping the campaign just [Pg 108] as it was accomplishing and successfully ending a year's work. It seems to have all come about through the misrepresentation of the Doolittle Peace Commission and the lack of proper information on the part of the Cabinet.

In the years 1863, 1864 and 1865 the Indians deliberately made war, believing that the Civil War had so crippled us that we could not effectively contend with them; but just as we had spent millions of dollars, sent thousands of troops into their country, and commenced fighting and capturing them, we were forced to lay down our arms almost in sight of the line of battle and beg for peace, and the Indians believed they had defeated us and that we could not conquer them, and for from three to ten years afterward we had to spend great sums, make winter campaigns, and suffer great losses of life and property, before we obtained the lasting peace which was in sight in 1865 and 1866 if we had been allowed to carry out our campaigns and plans to a legitimate end.

Upon the close of my campaigns on the plains the Legislature of the State of Iowa passed and sent me these commendations of my services:

Resolved, By the Senate and House of Representatives of the State of Iowa, That the thanks of the people of this State are due and are hereby extended to Major-General Grenville M. Dodge, for his able and efficient management of Indian affairs on the plains, in protecting the Great Overland Routes, and our western borders from the depredations and incursions of hostile Indians, as also for his distinguished services as a commander in the field, and his able administration of the Department of the Missouri.

During this campaigning on the plains I had as my escort Company A, Fourteenth Pennsylvania Cavalry. They belonged to one of the Regiments that was sent from the East to take part in the Indian campaigns, and did not ask to be mustered out until after the campaign. I was greatly indebted to this company for the close attention they gave to me and the intelligence they showed during the whole trip. They had served faithfully in the Civil War, and their veteran experience there was a great benefit in the work they had to do on the plains, often in taking messages and performing other duties where only two or three of them could be detailed at a time. It has always been a great pleasure to me to have had an invitation, ever since they organized their society, to attend their reunions, but, unfortunately, I have been so far away that I could not go; and to the surviving members I with great pleasure extend my thanks for their good services to me.

[Pg 109]

[Pg 110]

Model of fortified town on the table. Left to right—Lieutenant J. W. Barnes, A. D. C.; Captain O. J. Dodds, D. Q. M.; Captain C. C. Carpenter, Com. of Sub.; Captain J. K. King, A. Q. M.; Lieutenant-Colonel R. S. Barnhill, D. P. M.; Major N. B. Howard, Judge Advocate; Lieutenant J. H. Hogan, Ordnance Officer; Major W. R. Marsh, Medical Director; Captain B. P. Chenoweth, A. A. I. G.; Captain Henry Horn, Chief of Grand Guards.

[Pg 111]

CAMPAIGN UP THE TENNESSEE RIVER VALLEY

General Dodge
In the Rear of General Bragg's Army
And
Colonel Streight's Raid
Spring of 1863

When General Grant planned the second campaign against Vicksburg he notified me, then in command of the District of Corinth, with about eight thousand infantry and two thousand cavalry, that he intended to take my command with him; but a few days before starting he sent one of his staff officers to me stating that he had concluded to leave me with my command and some additional troops to hold that flank while he moved on Vicksburg. This dispatch was a great disappointment to myself and my command. When the officer returned to General Grant he no doubt told him of our disappointment, as General Grant wrote me a letter stating that my command was of much more importance than a command directly under him, and said he had fears that General Bragg, who was then facing General Rosecrans in Middle Tennessee, might detach a portion of his force, cross the Tennessee River, and endeavor to make a lodgment on the Mississippi River at some point and break up his communications with the North, with a view of forcing him to abandon the campaign. He said he had left me to take care of that flank, as he knew I would stay there. I read between the lines and learned what was expected of me.

General Grant, in discussing this order of his afterwards, said that he had learned from my services under him that I was peculiarly fitted for such a command, where I had to rely on my own judgment, and that I acted promptly without waiting for orders, and that it came, he thought, from my experience before the war, [Pg 112] when I was always in charge of engineering parties in the field and often in a hostile Indian country where I had to act promptly in any emergency. There was, at that time, quite a large force in my front and between me and General Bragg, commanded by General Earl Van Dorn, General N. B. Forrest, and General P. D. Roddey. This force was collecting supplies and storing them along the Memphis and Charleston Railroad from Bear River to Decatur, Ala. The Tennessee Valley in this territory was twenty miles wide, and full of all kinds of supplies. I wrote to General Grant about this storage of supplies for General Bragg's Army, and suggested that I move up the Tennessee Valley with my force to destroy these stores and whatever there was in the valley that Bragg's Army could utilize; but General Grant made no response then to my suggestion. In February I discovered a movement of the force in my front towards General Rosecrans's Army and notified him in the following dispatch:

Corinth, Miss., February 10, 1863.

Major-General Rosecrans:

One of my scouts left Van Dorn Sunday night. He then had two regiments and one battery across the Tombigbee, at Cotton-Gin Port; was crossing slowly, and all his forces had not got to him. His men and officers said he was going to Bragg. His stock is not in good condition. He appears to be going the Pikevill and Russellville road. Streams are high, and roads bad. We captured mail from Bragg's Army yesterday. All the officers' and privates' letters express a belief that Bragg is fixing to fall back; some say to Huntsville, some to Bridgeport. You can judge how reliable such suspicions are. I have endeavored to get a gunboat up to Florence, and if one could go there it could destroy all the forces, and check Van Dorn materially. I will co-operate with it in any way to benefit the service.

G. M. Dodge,
Brigadier-General.

On February 16th General Van Dorn's command commenced crossing the Tennessee to join General Bragg's Army. I sent my cavalry to attack him. I wired General Rosecrans that we had attacked Van Dorn's rear guard and took some fifty prisoners from him. He had with him General Roddey, commander of some fifteen hundred men, of which we captured about two hundred. These prisoners said they were ordered to join General Bragg's Army. General Rosecrans, in answer to my dispatch, sent me this message:

Murfreesborough, February 16, 1863.

Brigadier-General Dodge, Corinth, Miss.:

Hurlbut's request and my own coincide. Hope you will be able to cut off some of Van Dorn's command. Will give you all our news in your direction. Accept my thanks for your promptness and energy.

W. S. Rosecrans,
Major-General.

[Pg 113] Soon after this General Rosecrans conceived the idea of sending Colonel A. D. Streight with two thousand mounted cavalry and infantry from Nashville by boat to Eastport, Miss., to go from there east to Georgia, destroying the railroads and supplies Bragg's army was depending on, and then move south and west, finally landing in Corinth, Miss. General Rosecrans proposed that I should send two brigades to Iuka in support of this movement, which General Grant acceded to, and said in making this movement for me to go on and carry out the plan I had suggested in destroying the Memphis and Charleston Railroad and the supplies gathered along it. I sent this dispatch, giving my plan of the movement:

Hdqrs. Dist. of Corinth, Deprt. of the Tennessee,
Corinth, April 4, 1863.

Henry Binmore, Assistant Adjutant-General:

Captain:—In accordance with Major-General Hurlbut's dispatch, I submit the plan of operations east of here. General Rosecrans proposes to land a force at Florence, attack and take that place, while, with a heavy body of cavalry, he penetrates Alabama north of Tennessee River, and gets into Johnson's rear. At the same time I am to strike and take Tuscumbia, and, if practicable, push my cavalry to Decatur, destroy the saltpeter works, and the Tuscumbia and Decatur Railroad, which they have just finished, and take all the horses and mules in that country, to prevent them from raising any large crops. To do this, I propose to move simultaneously with General Rosecrans, throw all my cavalry suddenly across Bear Creek, capture the ferries, and hold them until my infantry and artillery arrive, and then immediately force my cavalry as far toward Tuscumbia as possible, and secure the crossings of Little Bear, on which creek the enemy will concentrate. To accomplish this I shall move light, taking nothing but ammunition and provisions, and march twenty miles per day, with infantry and artillery. I shall take such a force as to render certain the success of the expedition, and propose to take command in person. The movement is to be made next week, or as soon as General Rosecrans notifies me he is ready. I trust this will meet the view of the General commanding.

I am, very respectfully, your obedient servant,

G. M. Dodge,
Brigadier-General Commanding.

To ascertain what enemy I would have to meet, I sent my chief of staff, Captain George E. Spencer, a very competent officer who was a genius in getting inside of the enemy's lines, with a communication to General P. D. Roddey, who had returned to Tuscumbia, and was in command of the rebel forces south of the Tennessee River. I told Captain Spencer that the communication was an important one and he must not deliver it to any one except General Roddey; that he must impress upon the officer on the enemy's picket-line that he must take him to General Roddey and in that way he would be able to determine very closely what forces I would have to meet. Captain Spencer went prepared to do this. He met [Pg 114] the picket officer; they became very chummy, and the officer took Captain Spencer right through all of the enemy's forces between Bear River and Tuscumbia, and he delivered the message to General Roddey, who was in great anger at his officer; but they made the best of it. After the war, Captain Spencer and General Roddey were great friends and I believe partners in some business. The result of Captain Spencer's trip I set forth in the following dispatch to General Oglesby:

Corinth. *April* 17, 1863.

Major-General Oglesby, Jackson:

My A. A. G., Captain George E. Spencer, has just returned from Tuscumbia; succeeded in getting through all the enemy's camps and obtaining valuable information. The forces are posted as follows: Colonel Dibrell, 900 men, at Tuscumbia Landing; Colonel Josiah Patterson, 1,000, at Florence; Colonel M. W. Hannon, 1,800, at Tuscumbia; Colonel Roddey's old regiment, 800, at Tuscumbia Landing; Baxter Smith, 350, ten miles this side; Colonel Hampton, 300 at same place; W. R. Julian, 300, at Grey's, six miles this side; and Smith, 100, at Big Bear. The above all cavalry. Between Courtland and Tuscumbia, one brigade of infantry, under Colonel Wood, as follows: Colonel A. H. Helvenston, 300; Colonel J. B. Bibb, 500; Colonel W. B. Wood, Sixteenth Alabama, 400. The last brigade, and one brigade of cavalry, under General Roddey, arrived at Tuscumbia last week. This more than doubles their force. They have also five pieces of artillery at Florence and six pieces at Tuscumbia.

G. M. Dodge,
Brigadier-General.

Upon notification of General Rosecrans of the movement of Colonel Streight, I moved out to carry out the combined plan, engaging the enemy at Little Bear and Tuscumbia, and defeated them as my report shows. Colonel Streight was greatly delayed in starting from Nashville, and was only partially mounted, his intention being to complete the mount of his force as he traveled through the enemy's country — a fatal mistake. His delay in reaching me and my movement caused Bragg to send General Forrest to join General Roddey; and so by the time General Streight reached Eastport, April 21st, the force before me had been doubled and the best cavalry officer in the rebel force had arrived to take command in my front.

Colonel Streight lost part of his horses and mules while unloading at Eastport, and, although I made an effort to mount him, stripping my own transportation and scouring the country in my vicinity, still he left us after I captured Tuscumbia the second time, on May 26th, with two hundred of his men dismounted and one-half of the rest on mules, illy prepared for such a trip. I told Colonel Streight that I would hold the enemy in my front as long [Pg 115] as possible, but the moment Colonel Forrest got word of his movement he would go after him and follow him to death. His only salvation was to get three or four days' start by long marches before Forrest learned of his movement. Colonel Streight was an officer peculiarly fitted for such a raid. He was active, clearheaded, determined, and of excellent judgment, and his many fights with Forrest showed him full of resources; but his two-days' halt at Moulton, the heavy rains, and the condition of his stock, were fatal to him.

On the morning of May 27th I felt carefully of the enemy and found them in my front, and commenced immediately to force them back, trying to make them believe, if they discovered Colonel Streight, that it was only a side movement into the loyal part of Alabama, where we had many friends and where we enlisted a Regiment of loyal Alabamians, which was afterwards known as the First Alabama Cavalry, commanded by Colonel George E. Spencer, whose Regiment became noted for its valuable service throughout the war. General Sherman selected it as his headquarters escort in his march to the sea.

Generals Forrest and Roddey, on May 28th, made a determined stand to halt my advance on Town Creek. The high water delayed my crossing, but on the morning of the 29th, after my force had crossed and driven the enemy from the heights beyond, I discovered that I had only General Roddey and his force in my front and I forced my cavalry out towards Decatur until the enemy disappeared from the front. The evening of the 28th I notified Colonel Streight that Forrest was still with me, and I was greatly alarmed to find that Colonel Streight was still directly south of me, when I hoped he would be well on the road. When General Bragg found that I was continuing my advance up the Tennessee, destroying his stores, he despatched General Van Dorn with his cavalry command to cross the Tennessee at Florence and get in my rear, but as soon as the enemy disappeared in my front, I turned immediately and marched rapidly back to Bear River, so that, if General Van Dorn succeeded in crossing the Tennessee River, I would have him in my front. My troops destroyed all the supplies in the whole Valley of the Tennessee, burnt the railroad stations, and destroyed the railroad so that it was never rebuilt until after the war. There followed me back to Corinth almost the entire negro population of that valley. They came in every conceivable conveyance from their [Pg 116] masters' private carriage to a wheelbarrow, and they had hitched to the conveyances sometimes a cow and horse and sometimes a fine team of horses, or a cow and an ox. Hundreds were on foot, with their household goods packed on a mule, a horse, or a cow. They made a picturesque column, much longer than my command. At night their camps spread over a large territory, the camp-fires surrounded by the most motley and poorly-dressed crowd I ever saw, and it was a problem to me what I could do with them or what would become of them if the enemy's forces should happen to get into my rear. However, we all arrived safely at Corinth, where I established the great contraband camp and guarded it by two companies of Negro soldiers that I uniformed, armed, and equipped without any authority, and which came near giving me trouble. Many of the Negro men afterwards joined the First Alabama Colored Infantry and other Negro Regiments that I raised and mustered into the service.

In my advance up the Valley of the Tennessee, after I had passed Beaver Creek the enemy got into my rear, committing depredations and picking up stragglers, and all kinds of reports went back to Corinth of our fighting, capture, and other calamities too numerous to mention. These reports were all repeated to General Grant, who said, after being surfeited with them, "Well, if Dodge has accomplished what he started out to do, we can afford to lose him." General Grant said afterwards in discussing this movement that he knew they could not capture or destroy the kind of troops I had with me without my being heard from; that they might defeat me, but they could not capture me; and the boys used to use this saying in rounding up what value I was to the service. As my own report and that of Colonel Streight gives more and better detail of the movements of both, and the results, I submit them here:

I moved from Corinth with the Second Division, Sixteenth Army Corps, Wednesday, April 15. Camped at Burnsville. The next day moved to Cook's, two and a half miles west of Great Bear Creek, and made my preparations to cross, the rebels holding the opposite side.

Friday morning, April 17, I made a feint at Jackson and Bailings Fords, and, under the cover of my artillery, threw the most of my force across at Steminine's Ford.

The cavalry, under Colonel Cornyn, and mounted infantry, under Lieutenant-Colonel Phillips, made the crossing and pushed forward. My instructions were for them to go forward three and a half miles, and await my coming. Colonel Cornyn, meeting the enemy about a mile out, commenced fighting them, they falling back rapidly. Hearing of Colonel Roddey commanding a force of the enemy on my left flank, I sent orders [Pg 117] forward for the command to halt; but before the messenger got to him Colonel Roddey had got between the cavalry and infantry. The Third Brigade was in advance, commanded by Colonel Bane, who, ascertaining this fact, pushed forward and fell upon their rear, but not until Colonel Roddey had taken two pieces of artillery, twenty-two men, and one company of mounted infantry, who were guarding it, which, through neglect, had been allowed to fall three miles in the rear of the advance.

Colonel Cornyn, hearing firing in the rear, immediately fell back, and with the First Alabama Cavalry charged the rebels and retook the artillery and caissons, with the exception of one gun, which the enemy succeeded in getting off with.

The charge of the Alabamians with muskets only, and those not loaded, is creditable, especially as they are all new recruits and poorly drilled. In this charge, Captain Cameron, the commanding officer of the Alabama Cavalry, a deserving and much-lamented officer, was killed.

Colonel Bane, on his arrival, disposed of his troops admirably. Colonel Cornyn advanced with his cavalry as a feint, and the rebels advanced to meet him. He fell back to the rear of the infantry, which was posted under cover and out of sight on both flanks of the cavalry. On the appearance of the enemy, the infantry opened a heavy and destructive fire, which caused the rebels to fall back in confusion, utterly routed. This day's work brought us thirteen miles in advance of the main force.

Colonel Streight not arriving, I fell back with the advance to Great Bear Creek, where the rest of the command was posted, to await his coming.

Sunday afternoon, Colonel Streight commenced landing his force at Eastport, but came poorly prepared for his contemplated movement. He had two thousand infantry and about one thousand mules. At least four hundred of them were unserviceable, and in unloading them, through the carelessness of one of his officers, two hundred strayed away. He was under the impression that he would find plenty of stock in the valley to mount the rest and replace those broken down. During Monday and Tuesday we scoured the country, and found all we could.

Tuesday night Colonel Fuller's Brigade, from Corinth, joined me.

Wednesday morning I advanced with all the force, and came up with the enemy at Rock Cut, five miles west of Tuscumbia; planted my batteries, and drove them out of it, taking the line of Little Bear Creek that night. The enemy's position was a very strong one, and there was but one way to flank it. The enemy fell back as soon as I brought the infantry to bear upon them.

Thursday we moved, crossing at three places, throwing my cavalry by the Frankfort and Tuscumbia road, into the enemy's rear; but during the night, anticipating this movement, the enemy fell back. We reached Tuscumbia about noon, and after slight skirmishing took possession of the city. I immediately dispatched Lieutenant-Colonel Phillips, with two squadrons of mounted infantry, two squadrons of the Fifteenth Illinois Cavalry, and a section of Welker's battery, to take Florence. They refused to surrender, when Colonel Phillips immediately opened on the town. A few shell brought them to terms, and we occupied the place. At the same time I ordered Colonel Cornyn forward toward Courtland, to feel the enemy. He came up with their rear some two miles beyond Leighton. The command consisted on our part of the Tenth Missouri and Seventh Kansas Cavalry, about eight hundred in all, and drove the enemy eight miles. The rebel force was thirty-five hundred, besides one battery. The fighting of the cavalry against such odds is beyond all praise.

The next morning the cavalry fell back to Tuscumbia, to await the advance of the main column.

Finding it impossible to obtain stock to mount Colonel Streight's command, I took horses and mules from my teams and mounted infantry, and furnished him some six hundred head, mounting all but two hundred [Pg 118] of his men. I also turned over all my hard bread, some ten thousand rations, and he left me at midnight on the 26th instant, with the intention of going through Russellville, Moulton, and Blountsville, to Gadsden, then divide, one force to strike Rome and the other Etowah Bridge.

I moved forward Monday morning, and drove the enemy across Town Greek that night, and ascertained that they were in force, under Forrest, on the opposite bank. That night I communicated with Colonel Streight, at Mount Hope, and ascertained that he was all right.

Tuesday morning the creek rose ten feet, and the current was so swift that neither horse nor man could cross. I immediately made disposition to cross at three points, to cover the railroad bridge and throw across foot-bridges.

The resistance of the enemy was very strong, and their sharp-shooters very annoying. The artillery duel was very fine, parts of Welker's, Tannrath's, Richardson's, and Robinson's batteries taking part in it. The practice on both sides was excellent. The Parrott guns drove the enemy away from their pieces, disabling and keeping them away for two hours, but the fact of my being unable to cross infantry prevented our securing them.

About noon I crossed the railroad bridge with the Eighty-first O-hio and Ninth Illinois Infantry, and soon after crossed the rest of my force, except the artillery, on foot-bridges, and drove the enemy within three miles of Courtland, when they, hearing of the force at Moulton, fled to Decatur. I followed up, and then returned to camp at Town Creek that night, being unable to cross any of my artillery.

Colonel Streight reached Moulton Tuesday night, and commenced crossing the mountains Wednesday, having got nearly two days' start of them. They supposed he was making for Decatur, and only discovered Wednesday that he was crossing the mountains toward Georgia.

Having accomplished fully the object of the expedition, and driving the enemy, which was 5,500 strong, to Decatur, and having been on half rations for a week, I fell back to Tuscumbia, in order to communicate with transports, to obtain rations and ammunition. On arriving there I received information that the gunboats had gone down the river, taking the transports with them, a part of Van Dorn's force having made their appearance on the north side of the Tennessee River and shelled South Florence that day at 4 p. m. They also planted a battery at Savannah and Duck River; but my precaution in destroying all means of crossing the river on my advance, prevented him getting in my rear, and the gunboats, to save the transports, left the day before, having a short engagement at Savannah and Duck River. Van Dorn's force then moved toward Decatur. That was the last we heard of them.

On my return I burned all provisions, produce, and forage, all mills and tan-yards, and destroyed everything that would in any way aid the enemy. I took stock of all kinds that I could find, and rendered the valley so destitute that it cannot be occupied by the Confederates, except provisions and forage are transported to them. I also destroyed telegraph and railroad between Tuscumbia and Decatur, and all the ferries between Savannah and Courtland.

I have no doubt but that Colonel Streight would have succeeded had he been properly equipped and joined me at the time agreed upon. The great delay in an enemy's country necessary to fit him out gave them time to throw a large force in our front. Although Colonel Streight had two days' start, they can harass him, and perhaps check his movements long enough for them to secure all their important bridges. If he could have started from Bear Creek the day I arrived there, then my movements would have been so quick and strong that the enemy could not have got their forces together.

The animals furnished him were very poor at the start. Four hundred of them were used up before leaving me, and those furnished him by me [Pg 119] were about all the serviceable stock he had, though I hear he got two hundred good mules the day he left me, in Moulton Valley.

On my return, I sent Colonel Cornyn, with the Tenth Missouri, Seventh Kansas, Fifteenth Illinois Cavalry, and Ninth Illinois Mounted Infantry, to attack the force congregated at Tupelo and Okolona. He came up with the enemy on Wednesday, and immediately attacked them, they being some three thousand strong, under Major-General S. J. Gholson and Brigadier-General Ruggles. Brigadier-General Chalmers, with thirty-five hundred men, was at Pontotoc, but failed to come to Gholson's aid, though ordered to.

Colonel Cornyn fought so determinedly and so fast that he soon routed the force in his front, driving them in all directions, killing and wounding a large number and taking one hundred prisoners, including some seven officers; also a large number of arms and one hundred and fifty horses, saddles, etc.

The enemy fled toward Okolona and Pontotoc, and Colonel Cornyn returned to Corinth.

The expedition so far can be summed up as having accomplished the object for which it started, the infantry having marched two hundred and fifty miles and the cavalry some four hundred, and fought six successful engagements, driving the enemy, three thousand strong, from Bear Creek to Decatur, taking the towns of Tuscumbia and Florence, with a loss not to exceed one hundred, including three officers. Destroyed a million and a half bushels of corn, besides large quantities of oats, rye, and fodder, and five hundred thousand pounds of bacon. Captured one hundred and fifty prisoners, one thousand head of horses and mules, and an equal number of cattle, hogs, and sheep; also one hundred bales of cotton, besides keeping the whole command in meat for three weeks. Destroyed the railroad from Tuscumbia to Decatur; also some sixty flat-boats and ferries in the Tennessee River, thereby preventing Van Dorn, in his move, from crossing to my rear; also destroyed five tan-yards and six flouring-mills.

It has rendered desolate one of the best granaries of the South, preventing them from raising another crop this year, and taking away from them some fifteen hundred negroes.

We found large quantities of shelled corn, all ready for shipment, also bacon, and gave it to the flames.

I am, respectfully, your obedient servant,

G. M. Dodge,
Brigadier-General U. S. A.

The following is Colonel A. D. Streight's report:

General Dodge informed me that there was no doubt but Forrest had crossed the Tennessee River, and was in the vicinity of Town Creek; hence, he agreed to advance as far as Courtland, on the Decatur road, and, if possible, drive the enemy in that direction, but if they (the enemy) turned toward Moulton, our cavalry, under General Dodge, was to be sent in pursuit.

With this understanding, I marched from Tuscumbia at 11 p. m. on the night of the 26th instant in the direction of Moulton, via Russellville. It was raining very hard, and the mud and darkness of the night made our progress very slow. One hundred and fifty of my men had neither horses nor mules, and fully as many more had such as were unable to carry more than the saddles; hence fully three hundred of the men were on foot.

It was expected when I left General Dodge that the greater part of my command would be able to reach Moulton, some forty miles distant, by the next night, but, owing to the heavy rains and consequent bad condition of the roads, it was impossible; consequently I dispatched a messenger to General Dodge, stating that I would halt at Mount Hope and wait for the portion of my command who were on foot to come up.

[Pg 120] We continued to scour the country for horses and mules, but so many of those drawn at Nashville were continually failing, that, although we were successful in collecting a large number, still, many of the men were without anything to ride.

On the night of the 27th, at Mount Hope, I received word from General Dodge, stating that he had driven the enemy, and that I should push on. My command had not all come up yet, nor did they until about 10 a. m. the next day, when we proceeded to Moulton, where we arrived about dark. Up to this time we had been skirmishing occasionally with small squads of the enemy, but I could hear of no force of consequence in the country. All of the command but about fifty men were now mounted.

We started from Moulton, in the direction of Blountsville, via Day's Gap, about midnight on April 28. The two previous days it had been raining most of the time, and the roads were terrible, though on the evening of the 28th it bid fair for dry weather, which gave us strong hopes of better times.

We marched the next day (the 29th) to Day's Gap, about thirty-five miles, and bivouacked for the night. Every man now was mounted, and although many of the animals were very poor, nevertheless we had strong hopes that we could easily supply all future demands. We destroyed during the day a large number of wagons belonging to the enemy, laden with provisions, arms, tents, etc., which had been sent to the mountains to avoid us, but, luckily, they fell into our hands. We were now in the midst of devoted Union people. Many of Captain Smith's men (Alabamians) were recruited near this place, and many were the happy greetings between them and their friends and relations. I could learn nothing of the enemy in the country, with the exception of small squads of scouting-parties, who were hunting conscripts. We moved out the next morning before daylight. I will here remark that my men had been worked very hard in scouring so much of the country, and, unaccustomed as they were to riding, made it still worse; consequently, they were illy prepared for the trying ordeal through which they were to pass. I had not proceeded more than two miles, at the head of the column, before I was informed that the rear guard had been attacked, and just at that moment I heard the boom of artillery in the rear of the column. I had previously learned that the gap through which we were passing was easily flanked by gaps through the mountains, both above and below; consequently, I sent orders to the rear to hold the enemy in check until we could prepare for action. The head of the column was at the time on the top of the mountain. The column was moving through the gap; consequently the enemy was easily held in check.

I soon learned that the enemy had moved through the gaps on my right and left, and were endeavoring to form a junction in my advance; consequently I moved ahead rapidly until we passed the intersecting roads on either flank with the one we occupied. The country was open sand ridges, very thinly wooded, and afforded fine defensive positions. As soon as we passed the point above designated (about three miles from the top of the mountains), we dismounted and formed a line of battle on a ridge circling to the rear. Our right rested on a precipitous ravine and the left was protected by a marshy run that was easily held against the enemy. The mules were sent into a ravine to the rear of our right, where they were protected from the enemy's bullets. I also deployed a line of skirmishers, resting on our right and left flanks encircling our rear, in order to prevent a surprise from any detached force of the enemy that might approach us from that direction and to prevent any straggling of either stray animals or cowardly men.

In the meantime I had instructed Captain Smith, who had command of our rear guard (now changed to our front), to hold his position until the enemy pressed him closely, when he should retreat rapidly, and, if possible, draw them onto our lines, which were concealed by the men lying [Pg 121] down immediately back of the top of the ridge. The lines were left sufficiently open to permit Captain Smith's command to pass through near the center. I had two twelve-pounder mountain howitzers, which were stationed near the road (the center). They were also concealed. We had hardly completed our arrangements when the enemy charged Captain Smith in large force, following him closely, and no sooner had he passed our lines than our whole line rose up and delivered a volley at short range. We continued to pour a rapid fire into their ranks, which soon caused them to give way in confusion; but their reinforcements soon came up, when they dismounted, formed, and made a determined and vigorous attack. Our skirmishers were soon driven in, and about the same time the enemy opened upon us with a battery of artillery.

The enemy soon attempted to carry our lines, but were handsomely repulsed. During their advance they had run their artillery to within three hundred yards of our lines, and as soon as they began to waver I prepared for a charge. I ordered Colonel Hathaway, Seventy-third Indiana, and Lieutenant-Colonel Sheets, Fifty-first Indiana, on the left, to make a charge, in order to draw the attention of the battery, and immediately threw the Third Ohio, Colonel Lawson, and the Eightieth Illinois, Lieutenant-Colonel Rodgers, forward rapidly, hoping to capture the battery. The enemy, after a short but stubborn resistance, fled in confusion, leaving two pieces of artillery, two caissons, and about forty prisoners, representing seven different regiments, a larger number of wounded, and about thirty dead on the field. Among the former was Captain William H. Forrest, a brother of General Forrest. Our loss was about thirty killed and wounded, among the latter Lieutenant-Colonel Sheets, Fifty-first Indiana (mortally), a brave and gallant officer and one that we were illy prepared to lose, and Lieutenant Pavey, Eightieth Illinois (on my staff), severely.

It was now about 11 o'clock, fighting having continued since about 6 o'clock in the morning. I had learned, in the meantime, that the enemy were in heavy force, fully three times our number, with twelve pieces of artillery, under General Forrest in person; consequently I was fearful that they were making an effort to get around us and attack in the rear of our position; hence I decided to resume the march. Everything was soon in readiness, and we moved out, leaving a strong guard (dismounted) in the rear, to check any immediate advance the enemy might make previous to the column getting in motion. We were not too soon in our movements, for the column had hardly passed a cross-road some six miles from our first battle-ground when the enemy were discovered advancing on our left. Sharp skirmishing commenced at Crooked Creek, which is about ten miles south of Day's Gap, and finally the enemy pressed our rear so hard that I was compelled to prepare for battle. I selected a strong position about a mile south of the crossing of the creek, on a ridge called Hog Mountain. The whole force soon became engaged (about one hour before dark). The enemy strove first to carry our right; then charged the left; but with the help of the two pieces of artillery captured in the morning and the two mountain howitzers, all of which were handled with good effect by Major Vananda, of the Third Ohio, we were able to repulse them.

Fighting continued until about 10 p. m. when the enemy were driven from our front, leaving a large number of killed and wounded on the field. I determined at once to resume our march, and as soon as possible we moved out. The ammunition which we had captured with the two guns was exhausted, and being very short of horses, I ordered the guns spiked and the carriages destroyed. I had ordered the Seventy-third Indiana (Colonel Hathaway) to act as rear guard, and I remained in the rear in person, for the purpose of being at hand in case the enemy should attempt to press us as we were moving out. We had but fairly got under way when I received information of the enemy's advance.

The moon shone very brightly, and the country was an open woodland, [Pg 122] with an occasional spot of thick undergrowth. In one of these thickets I placed the Seventy-third Indiana, lying down, and not more than twenty paces from the road, which was in plain view. The enemy approached. The head of his column passed without discovering our position. At this moment the whole regiment opened a most destructive fire, causing a complete stampede of the enemy. I will here remark that the country from Day's Gap to Blountsville (about forty miles) is mostly uninhabited; consequently there is nothing in the country for man or beast. I had hopes that by pushing ahead we could reach a place where we could feed before the enemy would come up with us, and, by holding him back where there was no feed, compel him to lay over a day at least to recuperate. I had learned that they had been on a forced march from Town Creek, Ala., a day and two nights previous to their attacking us. We were not again disturbed until we had marched several miles, when they attacked our rear guard vigorously. I again succeeded in ambuscading them, which caused them to give up the pursuit for the night. We continued our march, and reached Blountsville about 10 o'clock in the morning. Many of our mules had given out, leaving their riders on foot, but there was very little straggling behind the rear guard.

At Blountsville we found sufficient corn to feed our tired and hungry animals. Ammunition and rations were hastily distributed to the men, and the remaining ammunition was put on pack-mules and the wagons burned, as it was now understood that it would be impossible to take them over the roads before us. After resting about two hours, we resumed our march in the direction of Gadsden.

The column had not got fairly under motion before our pickets were driven in, and a sharp skirmish ensued between Forrest's advance and our rear guard, under Captain Smith, in the town of Blountsville. The enemy followed closely for several miles, continually skirmishing with the rear guard, but were badly handled by small parties of our men stopping in the thick bushes by the side of the road and firing at them at short range, and when we reached the East Branch of the Black Warrior River the ford was very deep and the enemy pressed so closely that I was compelled to halt and offer him battle before we could cross. After some maneuvering, I advanced a heavy line of skirmishers, who drove the enemy out of sight of my main line, when I ordered the troops, except the skirmishers, to cross the river as rapidly as possible. After all had crossed except the skirmishers, they were rapidly withdrawn, under cover of our artillery, and a heavy line of skirmishers thrown out on the opposite bank for that purpose. It was about 5 p. m. when the last of the command crossed the East Branch of the Black Warrior. We proceeded in the direction of Gadsden without further interruption, with the exception of small parties who were continually harassing the rear of the column, until about 9 o'clock the next morning, May 2, when the rear guard was fiercely attacked at the crossing of Black Creek, near Gadsden. After a sharp fight the enemy was repulsed.

I had learned in the meantime, through my scouts, that a large column of the enemy was moving on our left, parallel with our route, evidently with the intention of getting in our front, which made it necessary for us to march all night, though the command was in no condition to do so, and, to add still more to my embarrassment, a portion of our ammunition had become damaged in crossing Will's Creek, which, at the time, was very deep fording. I only halted at Gadsden sufficiently long to destroy a quantity of arms and commissary stores found there, and proceeded on. Many of our animals and men were entirely worn out and unable to keep up with the column; consequently they fell behind the rear guard and were captured.

It now became evident to me that our only hope was in crossing the river at Rome and destroying the bridge, which would delay Forrest a day [Pg 123] or two and give us time to collect horses and mules, and allow the command a little time to sleep, without which it was impossible to proceed.

The enemy followed closely, and kept up a continuous skirmish with the rear of the column until about 4 p. m., at which time we reached Blount's plantation, about fifteen miles from Gadsden, where we could procure forage for our animals. Here I decided to halt, as it was impossible to continue the march through the night without feeding and resting, although to do so was to bring on a general engagement. Accordingly, the command was dismounted, and a detail made to feed the horses and mules, while the balance of the command formed in line of battle on a ridge southwest of the plantation.

Meanwhile the rear guard, in holding the enemy in check, had become severely engaged and was driven in. The enemy at once attacked our main line, and tried hard to carry the center, but were gallantly met and repulsed by the Fifty-first and Seventy-third Indiana, assisted by Major Vananda, with two mountain howitzers. They then made a determined effort to turn our right, but were met by the gallant Eightieth Illinois, assisted by two companies of the Third Ohio.

The enemy, with the exception of a few skirmishers, then fell back to a ridge some half a mile distant, and commenced massing his force, as if preparing for a more determined attack. It was becoming dark, and I decided to withdraw unobserved, if possible, and conceal my command in a thicket some half a mile to our rear, there to lie in ambush and await his advance. In the meantime I had ordered Captain Milton Russell (Fifty-first Indiana) to take two hundred of the best-mounted men, selected from the whole command, and proceed to Rome, and hold the bridge until the main command could come up.

The engagement at Blount's plantation revealed the fact that nearly all of our remaining ammunition was worthless, on account of having been wet. Much of that carried by the men had become useless by the paper wearing out and the powder sifting away. It was in this engagement that the gallant Colonel Hathaway (Seventy-third Indiana) fell, mortally wounded, and in a few moments expired. Our country has seldom been called upon to mourn the loss of so brave and valuable an officer. His loss to me was irreparable. His men had almost worshiped him, and when he fell it cast a deep gloom of despondency over his regiment which was hard to overcome.

We remained in ambush but a short time when the enemy, who by some means had learned of our whereabouts, commenced a flank movement, which we discovered in time to check. I then decided to withdraw as silently as possible, and push on in the direction of Rome, but as a large number of the men were dismounted, their animals having given out, and the remainder of the stock was so jaded, tender-footed, and worn down, our progress was necessarily slow; yet, as everything depended on our reaching Rome before the enemy could throw a sufficient force there to prevent our crossing the bridge, every possible effort was made to urge the command forward. We proceeded without interruption until we reached the vicinity of Centre, when one of my scouts informed me that a force of the enemy was posted in ambush but a short distance in our front. I immediately threw forward a line of skirmishers, with orders to proceed until they were fired upon, when they should open a brisk fire on the enemy, and hold their position until the command had time to pass.

The plan worked admirably, for, while my skirmishers were amusing the enemy, the main column made a detour to the right, and struck the main road some three miles to the rear of the enemy. As soon as our main force had passed, the skirmishers withdrew and fell in the rear of the column. I was then hopeful that we could reach Rome before the enemy could overtake us. My principal guide had thus far proved reliable, and I had made particular inquiries of him as to the character of the road [Pg 124] and the country the evening before, and he assured me that there were no difficult streams to cross and that the road was good; hence we approached the Chattanooga River at the ferry without any information as to the real condition of things. Captain Russell had managed to ferry the last of his command across about one hour previous to my arrival, but the enemy had seized and run off the boat before we reached there.

I then ascertained that there was a bridge some seven or eight miles up the river, near Gaylesville, and procured new guides and pushed on as rapidly as possible in order to reach the bridge before the enemy should take possession of it. We had to pass over an old coal-chopping for several miles, where the timber had been cut and hauled off for charcoal, leaving innumerable wagon-roads running in every direction, and the command was so worn out and exhausted that many were asleep, and in spite of every exertion I could make, with the aid of such of my officers as were able for duty, the command became separated and scattered into several squads, traveling in different directions, and it was not until near daylight that the last of the command had crossed the river. The bridge was burned, and we proceeded on and passed Cedar Bluff just after daylight. It now became evident that the horses and mules could not reach Rome without halting to rest and feed. Large numbers of the mules were continually giving out. In fact, I do not think that at that time we had a score of the mules drawn at Nashville left, and nearly all of those taken in the country were barefooted, and many of them had such sore backs and tender feet that it was impossible to ride them; but, in order to get as near as possible to the force I had sent ahead, we struggled on until about 9 a. m. when we halted and fed our animals. The men, being unaccustomed to riding, had become so exhausted from fatigue and loss of sleep that it was almost impossible to keep them awake long enough to feed. We had halted but a short time, when I was informed that a heavy force of the enemy was moving on our left, on a route parallel with the one we were marching on, and was then nearer Rome than we were. About the same time I received this information our pickets were driven in. The command was immediately ordered into line, and every effort made to rally the men for action, but nature was exhausted, and a large portion of my best troops actually went to sleep while lying in line of battle under a severe skirmish-fire. After some maneuvering, Forrest sent in a flag of truce, demanding the surrender of my forces. Most of my regimental commanders had already expressed the opinion that, unless we could reach Rome and cross the river before the enemy came up with us again, we should be compelled to surrender. Consequently, I called a council of war. I had learned, however, in the meantime that Captain Russell had been unable to take the bridge at Rome. Our condition was fully canvassed. As I have remarked before, our ammunition was worthless, our horses and mules in a desperate condition, the men were overcome with fatigue and loss of sleep, and we were confronted by fully three times our number, in the heart of the enemy's country, and, although personally opposed to surrender, and so expressed myself at the time, yet I yielded to the unanimous voice of my regimental commanders, and at once entered into negotiations with Forrest to obtain the best possible terms I could for my command, and at about noon, May 3, we surrendered as prisoners of war.

We were taken to Richmond, Va. The men were soon sent through the lines and exchanged. My officers and myself were confined in Libby Prison, where we remained until the night of February 9 last, when four of my officers and myself, together with several other prisoners, succeeded in making our escape, and reached Washington in safety about March 1. The balance of my officers, or nearly all of them, are still confined as prisoners or have died of disease the result of long confinement, insufficient food, and cruel treatment at the hands of the enemy.

I am unable to report the exact number of casualties in the command, [Pg 125] but from the best information I have been able to obtain there were fifteen officers and about one hundred and thirty enlisted men killed and wounded. It was a matter of astonishment to all that so much fighting should occur with so few casualties on our side; but we acted purely on the defensive, and took advantage of the nature of the country as best we could. From actual personal observation where we had driven the enemy from the field, and from what my surgeons, left with our wounded, learned in relation to the loss of the enemy, I am convinced that we killed more of his men than we lost in both killed and wounded.

Previous to the surrender, we had captured and paroled about two hundred prisoners, and had lost about the same number in consequence of the animals giving out, and the men, unable to keep up, broke down from exhaustion, and were necessarily picked up by the enemy; but in no case was the enemy able to capture a single man in any skirmish or battle within my knowledge.

I deem it proper to mention the barbarous treatment my wounded received at the hands of the enemy. Owing to the nature of the service we were performing, we were compelled to leave our wounded behind. I provided for them as best I could by leaving them blankets and such rations as we had, and two of my surgeons remained behind to attend them; but no sooner did the enemy get possession of our hospitals than they robbed both officers and men of their blankets, coats, hats, boots, shoes, rations, and money. The medical stores and instruments were taken from the surgeons, and my wounded left in a semi-naked and starving condition, in some instances many miles from any inhabitants, to perish.

Many thanks to the Union ladies of that country, for they saved many a brave soldier from a horrible death.

In reviewing the history of this ill-fated expedition, I am convinced that had we been furnished at Nashville with 800 good horses, instead of poor, young mules, we would have been successful, in spite of all other drawbacks; or if General Dodge had succeeded in detaining Forrest one day longer, we would have been successful even with our poor outfit.

A. D. Streight,
Colonel Fifty-first Indiana Veteran Volunteer Infantry.

On my return, I dispatched Colonel Cornyn with his Brigade to the attack of the force of the enemy that I had located near Tupelo, Miss. He tells the story of his battle better than I can, in his official report, which follows:

We arrived at Tupelo on Tuesday, May 5, and here we fought the best-contested fight of the whole expedition. Just before entering the town of Tupelo, and to the east of the railroad, it is necessary to cross a dense and almost impassable swamp, on the western edge of which runs Old Town Creek. We had almost reached the western edge, and were approaching, as well as the nature of the swamp would permit, the bridge over this creek, when the enemy, entirely unseen by us, opened upon us with musketry. I immediately threw out to my right and left several squadrons of the Tenth Missouri, who succeeded in dislodging the enemy, and securing an easy passage of the bridge for the balance of the command. Still keeping my skirmishers out to my right and left, and an advance guard in front,

I moved down a lane to the left and south of the town and massed my command in an open field, about six hundred yards from the southern border of Tupelo. Here word was brought me from one of my skirmishing squadrons that the enemy were drawn up in line on their front, to the number of six hundred. I ordered two squadrons of the Seventh Kansas, that were armed with Colt's revolving rifles, to dismount and attack them on foot, supporting them with two squadrons of the Tenth Missouri (mounted), [Pg 126] under Lieutenant-Colonel Bowen, with orders to charge with the saber as soon as the enemy's line should break. This order, I am proud to say, was well obeyed and gallantly executed by both the mounted and dismounted soldiers, for the enemy retired, and for a few minutes all was silent along the lines. In about half an hour from the first attack, sharp firing was heard on my front, and the enemy was advancing toward us with yells. I immediately moved my whole force to the rear and west of the village, and, placing my mountain howitzers upon the brow of a hill, I sent forward all the cavalry except one squadron of the Fifteenth Illinois, which I ordered to dismount and support the battery. Lieutenant-Colonel Phillips, commanding the Ninth Illinois Mounted Infantry, having been detailed for that purpose early in the morning, acted as the rear guard and guard for the train, and, knowing that the rear was in such good hands, I felt no anxiety on that account; and this important trust was well sustained. As soon as my front had become fully engaged with the enemy, who fought with considerable determination, I ordered the battery to shell the woods from which the enemy was emerging. This fire was effective, and from that moment the battle became general. At one time two regiments of mounted infantry, commanded by the rebel General Ruggles, forced their way between my fighting column and my reserve, but were suddenly induced to retire much more rapidly than they came. My left at one time fell back toward the battery, which then poured charge after charge of canister into the rebel ranks, with considerable effect, forcing them to retreat, rapidly followed by the cavalry. The enemy had scarcely begun to waver when his whole force fled in dismay, throwing away their arms, coats, and hats. We took from the enemy eighty-one prisoners, including three commissioned officers. On the field, the scene of the battle, immense quantities of arms, coats, and blankets were found and destroyed by us. I had no means of ascertaining the enemy's loss in killed and wounded, but from the evidence of the battle-field it must have been heavy.

Florence M. Cornyn,
Colonel Tenth Missouri Cavalry, Commanding Cavalry Brigade.

Colonel Cornyn was a very efficient cavalry officer and always accomplished whatever he was sent to do. He was an aggressive fighter, always attacking, no matter what the force before him, and had won a deserved standing as a Brigade commander. When he was killed, by his Lieutenant-Colonel, Bowen, during the latter's trial before a court-martial on charges preferred by Colonel Cornyn, there was a bitter personal dispute and enmity between them which came to this sad ending.

[Pg 127]

[Pg 128]

ARMY AND CORPS COMMANDERS OF THE ARMY OF THE TENNESSEE

Left to Right—Front Row, Major-General W. T. Sherman, Major-General U. S. Grant, Major-General James B. McPherson, Major-

General O. O. Howard. Rear row, Major-General John A. Logan, Major-General G. M. Dodge, Major-General Frank P. Blair. Extreme right, Brigadier-General John A. Fuller, leading Division of the Sixteenth Army Corps. Copy of painting by James E. Taylor for Major-General W. T. Sherman.

[Pg 129]

THE ARMY OF THE TENNESSEE

Address to the Army of the Tennessee Delivered at the National Encampment, G. A. R. Washington, D. C., October, 1902 By Major-general Grenville M. Dodge

Comrades of the Army of the Tennessee:

On the 28th of August, 1861, General U. S. Grant was assigned to duty in command of the District of Southeast Missouri, with headquarters at Cairo, Ill., and here commenced the organization and growth of the Army of the Tennessee. It remained under his personal command, or as a unit of his great Army, from the beginning until the end of the war, except for two short intervals, one after the great Battle of Donelson, and the other after the greater Battle of Shiloh, both of which he won, and gave the first great light and hope to our country; and it is hard now, after reading all the records, to understand the reasons for his being relieved. It appears to have been done through a misunderstanding, and with no intention of doing injustice to General Grant.

Following General Grant as commander came General Sherman, a member of the Army almost as long as General Grant. General Sherman was in direct command, or the Army served under him as a unit of his greater Army, from the time he assumed command until the end of the war.

After General Sherman came General McPherson, that ideal soldier, who commanded the Army until he fell in the great Battle of Atlanta, on the 22d of July. Upon his death, General Logan took command of the Army, as the senior officer present, and at the end of the battle of July 22d he could say that he had met and defeated Hood's whole Army in the greatest battle of that campaign.

Following General Logan came General O. O. Howard, the only General taken from another Army to command it in all the history of the Army of the Tennessee, or even any of its Corps. [Pg 130] The next day after assuming command General Howard led the Army into the great battle of the 28th of July, which the Confederates said was not a battle, but a simple killing and slaughtering of their forces. He remained in command until the end of the Rebellion, and at the end of the war generously gave way to General Logan, so that one of its original members might command it at the great review here in Washington—an act that could come only from such a just and thoughtful soldier as Howard.

I speak of our Army's commanders first, as an Army takes its habits and character from its head; and probably no other Army in the world was so fortunate as to have always at its head great soldiers and great commanders, recognized as such the world over—two of them the peers of any commander that ever stood up in a great conflict.

The Army of the Tennessee covered more ground in its campaigns than all the other Armies combined, and all its campaigns were marked by some great struggle, battle, or movement that challenged the admiration of the world. First came Fort Donelson, next Vicksburg, and following that Chattanooga, where it fought on both flanks in that great battle, one Division taking the point of Lookout Mountain above the clouds. Then came the Atlanta campaign; following that the strategical march to the sea; and, finally, that bold movement from Savannah to Goldsboro, which is considered by the best critics as one of the boldest and best-planned campaigns of history—one in which every chance was taken, and every opportunity given the enemy to concentrate upon an inferior force.

The record of this Army is probably the most satisfactory of any that ever existed, as it was harmonious in all its parts and had no jealousies, each of its units to the best of its ability helping the others. Again, it was modest; it struck blow after blow, and let the world sing its praises. All its campaigns were great successes, and it never lost a battle. All its Army, Corps, Division, and Brigade commanders were exceptionally able men, and were seldom relieved except to assume more important commands. Its experiences were more varied than any other Army, for in its campaigns, battles, and marches, reaching from the Missouri River to the Atlantic, at Washington, over a territory two thousand miles long and five hundred miles wide, it opened the Mississippi, it forced its way to the sea, it was reviewed by the Government of the nation here in this city, and it disbanded and the men went to their homes [Pg 131] without causing an unpleasant comment or a painful thought in all this broad land.

The Society of the Army of the Tennessee is endeavoring to perpetuate its history and memories by erecting here in this capital of our great nation monuments to the memory of its dead commanders which will place before the world not only their deeds, but the great events in which our Army took so important a part. First came General McPherson, as he was the first to fall, in the great Battle of Atlanta. He fell just after watching the attack in the rear on the Sixteenth Army Corps, which held the key to the situation. He was a dear friend of mine; and the last words he spoke were in praise of the fighting of that Corps. General Sherman, in reporting his death, spoke of him as follows:

General McPherson fell in battle, booted and spurred, as the gallant and heroic gentleman should wish. Not his the loss, but the country's, and the army will mourn his death and cherish his memory as that of one who, though comparatively young, had risen by his merit and ability to the command of one of the best armies which the nation had called into existence to vindicate her honor and integrity. History tells of but few who so blended the grace and the gentleness of the friend with the dignity, courage, faith and manliness of the soldier. His public enemies, even the men who directed the fatal shot, never spoke or wrote of him without expressions of marked respect. Those whom he commanded loved him even to idolatry, and I, his associate and commander, fail in words adequate to express my opinion of his great worth.

General McPherson was so dear to our old Army that the great victory at the Battle of Atlanta was never spoken of by our Army except to express our great grief at the loss of our commander. His faith in what he could accomplish with our Army was unbounded. He spoke of us on July 4, 1863, as follows:

With tireless energy, with sleepless vigilance, by night and by day, with battery and with rifle-pits, with trench and mine, you made your sure approaches, until, overcome by fatigue and driven to despair in the attempt to oppose your irresistible progress, the whole garrison of over 30,000 men, with all their arms and munitions of war, have, on this, the anniversary of our National Independence, surrendered to the invincible troops of the Army of the Tennessee. The achievements of this hour will give a new meaning to this memorable day, and Vicksburg will brighten the glow of the patriot's heart which kindles at the mention of Bunker Hill and Yorktown. This is indeed an auspicious day for you. The God of Battle is with you. The dawn of a conquered peace is breaking upon you. The plaudits of an admiring world will hail you wherever you go, and it will be an ennobling heritage, surpassing all riches, to have been of the Army of the Tennessee on the Fourth of July, 1863.

Next we erected the statue, facing Pennsylvania Avenue, of General John A. Rawlins, who, above all, represented the organization and spirit of our great Army, and who shared its fortunes [Pg 132] from beginning to end as Chief of Staff of its first and greatest commander. In 1873, upon the death of General Rawlins, General John A. Logan spoke of him thus:

But there is one whose tongue is now still in death whose name I cannot forbear to mention; one who, though gone from our midst, is with us in memory: for who can forget John A. Rawlins? Faithful in every duty, true in every trust, though dead he is not forgotten; though gone forever, yet he will ever live in affectionate remembrance in the hearts of all who knew him. His name is woven in indelible colors in the history of our country, and is linked with a fame that is undying.

General Rawlins, in giving a history of the Army of the Tennessee, paid this tribute to it:

In no army did the soldier enjoy greater liberty, consistent with military discipline, than in the Army of the Tennessee, and in none were his rights and his life more carefully guarded.

The subordination of the Army of the Tennessee to the policies and acts of the Government affecting the institution of slavery in the prosecution of the war, is worthy of the highest commendation. It had no policy of its own to propose, but went forth, as expressed by the legislative branch of the Government, to do battle in no spirit of oppression, or for any purpose of conquest or subjugation, or purpose of overthrowing or interfering with the rights or established institutions of the States in rebellion; but to defend and maintain the supremacy of the constitution, and to preserve the Union with all the dignity, equality and rights of the several States unimpaired.

The Army of the Tennessee did great deeds in all the departments of the States' service, and individually and collectively illustrated in a peculiar manner the qualities of noble American character which gained success in the field, preserved its fruits by subsequent statesmanship, and by exalted virtue crowned victory with the attributes of peace and justice.

In April, 1900, we unveiled the beautiful and life-like monument to General John A. Logan, that brilliant, magnetic soldier, our comrade from Cairo to Louisville. Of him, at the unveiling, President McKinley spoke as follows:

Logan's career was unique. His distinction does not rest upon his military achievements alone. His services in the Legislature of his own State, in the National House of Representatives, and in the Senate of the United States, would have given him an equally conspicuous place in the annals of the country. He was great in the forum and in the field.

He came out of the war with the highest military honors of the volunteer soldier. Brilliant in battle and strong in military council, his was also the true American spirit, for when the war was ended he was quick and eager to return to the peaceful pursuits of civil life.

General Logan's love and devotion to us only ended with his life, and at one of our reunions he characterized our work thus:

The Army of the Tennessee was not limited in its scope; the theater of its operations and the extent of its marches, comprehending within their bounds an area greater than Greece and Macedonia in their palmiest days, and greater than most of the leading kingdoms of Europe at the present day, reached from the Missouri River on the north nearly to the Gulf of Mexico on the south, and from the Red River of Louisiana to the Atlantic Ocean.

[Pg 133] The friendship and loyalty of Sherman to Grant was the first great cause of the success of both, and for the harmony that existed in the Army of the Tennessee. Sherman fell under the command of Grant at Paducah, in the spring of 1862, holding a small command. He was the ideal soldier, as he dropped from a Department and Army commander to that of a post, and later a Division, without a murmur. Sherman's first words to Grant, on February 15, 1862, were these:

I should like to hear from you, and will do everything in my power to hurry forward to you reinforcements and supplies, and if I could be of service myself would gladly come without making any question of rank with you or General Smith, whose commissions are of the same date.

On the same date he wrote again:

Command me in any way. I feel anxious about you, as I know the great facilities they [the enemy] have of concentration, by means of the river and railroads, but have faith in you.

The monument to our old commander, General Sherman, is nearly complete. It is upon these grounds we expect to unveil it next October, and, as President of the Society of the Army of the Tennessee, and as President of the Commission which has in charge the erection of the monument, I give you a cordial invitation to be present. You will receive due notice, and proper arrangements will be made for the occasion, and you will meet here your comrades of the Armies of the Cumberland, the Potomac, and the Ohio, who have already signified their intention of being present to honor the memory of our old commander.

And now, my comrades, it is with the greatest satisfaction that I say to you that after seven years' continued effort, this year we obtained an appropriation from Congress of $250,000 to be used in the erection of a monument upon these grounds to General U. S. Grant, (and the model for it will soon be selected,) to this modest, charitable, and just soldier and statesman. The whole world has given its tribute. From those whom we fought and defeated have come the most gallant words of praise and touching sympathy. President Lincoln, above all others, recognized his power and ability when he handed him his commission and gave him command of all the Armies, and assured him that he should not in any way interfere with him,—armed him with all the powers of the President, with *carte blanche* to use them as he saw fit. Grant made his answer at Appomattox, bringing peace to our nation and gratitude to the conquered. General Grant was a man of few words, and when [Pg 134] called upon to speak of the Army of the Tennessee, paid it this tribute:

As an Army, the Army of the Tennessee never sustained a single defeat during four years of war. Every fortification which it assailed surrendered. Every force arrayed against it was either defeated, captured, or destroyed. No officer was ever assigned to the command of that Army who had afterwards to be relieved from it, or to be reduced to another command. Such a history is not accident.

And now, my comrades, one of our number who has left us by an assassin's hand, whose heart, words and acts were ever for us, who from a Major in our Army became the best-loved President of our nation, Comrade William McKinley, at one of our gatherings paid this tribute to you:

It is recorded that in eighteen months' service the Army of the Tennessee captured 80,000 men, with flags and arms, including 600 guns—a greater force than was engaged on either side in the terrible battle of Chickamauga. From the fields of triumph in the Mississippi Valley it turned its footsteps towards the eastern seaboard, brought relief to the forces at Chattanooga and Nashville, pursued that peerless campaign from Atlanta to the seaboard under the leadership of the glorious Sherman, and planted the banners of final victory on the parapets of Fort McAllister.

It is said that the old Army of the Tennessee never lost a battle and never surrendered a flag. Its Corps badges—"forty rounds" of the Fifteenth Corps; the fleeting arrow of the Seventeenth Corps; the disc, from which four bullets have been cut, of the Sixteenth Corps—are all significant of the awful business of cruel war, all of them suggestive of the missiles of death.

It gave the Federal Army Grant, Sherman, and Sheridan; McPherson, Howard, Blair, Logan, Hazen, John E. Smith, C. F. Smith, Halleck, Rawlins, Prentiss, Wallace, Porter, Force, Leggett, Noyes, Hickenlooper, C. C. Walcutt, and your distinguished President, who flamed out the very incarnation of soldierly valor before the eyes of the American people; all have a secure place in history and a secure one in the hearts of their countrymen.

On this anniversary, as my closing words to you, two verses of General John Tilson's tribute are most appropriate:

> Ho! comrades of the brave old band, we gather here once more,
> With smiling eye and clasping hand, to fight our battles o'er.
> To quaff from out the brimming cup of old-time memory,
> And bright relight the pathway of our old Tennessee.
> As myriad sparks of war's romance our meetings warm inspire;
> The heady fight, the anxious march, the jolly bivouac fire;
> The days of doubt, of hope, of care, of danger, and of glee;
> Oh, what a world of racy thought illumines Tennessee!
>
> Our roster thins; as years pass on we drop off one by one;
> Ere long, too soon, to yearly call, there will be answer—none;
> Then as along the record page these mourning columns creep,
> The whisper comes to closer still our living friendships keep.
> Another thought we forward cast to that not distant day,
> When left of all our gallant band will be one veteran gray,
> And here's to him who meets alone—wherever he may be,
> The last, the lone survivor of the grand old Tennessee.

MAJOR-GENERAL G. M. DODGE AND STAFF

Commanding the Army and Department of the Missouri.

Front Row — Colonel T. J. Haines, U. S. A., C. S.; Major-General G. M. Dodge; Colonel William Myers, U. S. A., Q. M.; Colonel James H. Baker, Tenth Minnesota, P. M. G. Back Row — Colonel Benjamin L. W. Bonneville, U. S. A. (retired), C. S. of Musters, age 72; Captain William Holcke, A. D. C, Chief of Engineers; Major J. F. Randolph, U. S. A., Surgeon; Captain Frank Enos A. A. G.; Colonel John V. Dubois, A. D. C, Inspector-General; Lieutenant Edward Jonas, Fiftieth Illinois, A. D. C.; Major John W. Barnes, A. A. G.; Major Lucien Eaton, Judge Advocate; Lieutenant George C. Tichenor, A. D. C.

THE CAMPAIGN IN THE WEST

Address to the Army of the South-West at National Encampment, G. A. R. Washington, D. C. October, 1902

My connection with the United States forces west of the Mississippi River commenced at the beginning of the war, when I took my Regiment, the Fourth Iowa, to St. Louis, and fell under the command of Fremont. I took part in the campaigns of that Department until after the Battle of Pea Ridge, when I left the command and went to the Army of the Tennessee. After the Atlanta campaign, in November, 1864, I returned to Missouri as commander of that Department and Army.

Of the transactions of the troops south of Missouri I have very little knowledge; but I know that the troops which served west of the Mississippi never had credit for the amount of work, hardships and exposures they endured. Owing to the fact of there having been fought there but two great battles, Wilson's Creek and Pea Ridge, and two minor ones, what they did was swallowed up in the great events that occurred east of the Mississippi. Even Pope's campaign opening up a portion of the Mississippi is hardly ever spoken of.

The Battle of Wilson's Creek, the first signal contest west of the Mississippi, was fought before my command reached St. Louis. The history of that battle, and the credit that is due to the commander of that Army, General Lyon, and his men, are well known. There participated in the battle many officers who were afterwards greatly distinguished; among them Schofield, Sturgis, Hunter, and others. It was the first battle that called attention to the West, and to the troops west of the Mississippi. That battle was lost because a portion of the command did not comprehend and fulfill General Lyon's orders. This mistake would have been overcome if [Pg 138] it had not been for the loss in the battle of its commander, General Lyon. But the fighting of the troops and the boldness of the movement immediately attracted the attention of the country, and held it until after the battle of Pea Ridge.

The Army of the Southwest, which General Curtis commanded, and which traveled three hundred miles from its base without water or rail communication, and lived off a barren country, and which fought that decisive Battle of Pea Ridge and cleared the country until nearly the end of the war of any organized force of the enemy, had more marching and endured more suffering than the great Armies I was connected with east of the Mississippi, and its three days' fighting at Pea Ridge compared favorably with any of our battles, when the numbers engaged are considered.

Then again, at the end of the war, the sufferings of the troops that I took onto the plains in the Indian campaigns in the winters of 1864-5, 1865-6, were far beyond any of the sufferings of any of our Armies during the Civil War. Their exposures through the cold weather, and the brutalities and butcheries of the Indians, which it was impossible for them to avenge or retaliate, were beyond description.

Our early campaign in Missouri was without previous experience. It was simply one soldier standing up against another in battle, and we had to learn all the tricks of camp life, and from experience how to take care of our soldiers.

There were a great many funny incidents in the Pea Ridge campaign. The Southwestern Army was organized at Rolla, Missouri, of which post I was in command. My quartermaster was Captain Philip H. Sheridan, and my commissary, Captain M. P. Small. No one who knew or saw Sheridan then thought of the great position he was to occupy in our Army, but when he took hold of that Army and stripped it and fed it, three hundred miles away from rail or water communication, we all knew that his was a master-mind. When he came to me at Rolla, the first order he gave was to take away about three-quarters of our transportation. I think we had about two wagons to the company, and he brought us down to about four to a regiment. You can all appreciate the rebellion I had on my hands when I undertook to enforce his order. I know he stood by and watched to see what I was going to do. Every Regiment and Command entered a protest, and said some very unkind things of him, denouncing him as a regular officer who [Pg 139] had no mercy upon a volunteer; but I had then had experience enough to appreciate our necessities, and started in by stripping my own Regiment, and then enforcing the orders upon the others. We were not long on that march before they appreciated the foresight of Sheridan. He had great energy and great resources. He had to run all the mills along our line of march; he had to forage in every direction, and the punishment that he gave to some of the people to make them tell where their horses, forage and sweet potatoes were hidden would astonish those of our people who have been so horrified at the mild persuasions used for similar purposes in the Philippines.

To show you how little we knew of war on our first march, in January, 1862, from Rolla to Springfield, Missouri, all the reports we had obtained were that Price and his Army were in Springfield. The troops of our Army were divided into two commands, those under Siegel, composed of two Divisions, commanded by Osterhaus and Asboth, mostly Germans, and two Divisions of Americans commanded by Colonel Jeff C. Davis and Colonel E. A. Carr. I commanded a Brigade on the extreme left in Carr's Division, and, in accordance with instructions, put out a company in front of me as skirmishers. It was dark, and impossible for us to see much, and the first thing I knew I had lost my skirmishers, and was in great distress until about daylight in the morning, when, while Siegel's guns and our own were booming away at Springfield, my company came back mounted on Confederate horses and mules — old hacks that the enemy had left behind them — and brought us news that there was no enemy in Springfield, and had not been for two or three days.

As we marched along towards Pea Ridge through the country, Price's Army faced us with a rear guard only, his main body keeping a long distance ahead of us. At every stream they would halt our advance, and move out a couple of pieces of their artillery, and put out a strong skirmish-line, which would force our Army into line, thinking we were going to have a battle. My Brigade led the advance most of the time on that march, and as soon as they would line up the officers would have the boys strip. They would throw down their chickens, sweet potatoes, and everything they had gathered, and by the time they had gone forward, and the enemy had run, the Thirty-sixth Illinois, or some other Regiment, would come up and gobble what they had left. About the third time we lined up I discovered that every boy was hanging on to his chickens, sweet potatoes, and provender, and when I gave orders to the Colonels to have them throw them aside, the boys made answer: "No you don't, Colonel! You can't fool us any more; we have fed those Thirty-sixth Illinois fellows as long as we propose to."

[Pg 140]

FORT COTTONWOOD

Afterwards Fort McPherson, in the Indian Campaign, 1865. The fort was one hundred miles west of Fort Kearney, and was originally occupied as a trading post by Sylvanus Dodge, father of General Dodge.

[Pg 141] At Pea Ridge we were surrounded by Van Dorn, who placed Price's two Divisions in our rear, and he himself on our right flank with McCullough and McIntosh's Divisions. The great Pea Ridge divided his Army, so it was impossible for one part to support the other. His Army was twice as large as that of Curtis, and the fact that it was divided enabled Curtis to whip his Army in detail, so that Van Dorn's Army was virtually whipped before Curtis got his entire force into the field, Siegel only coming into battle after Van Dorn's Arkansas force had left for the South, Jeff C. Davis's Division having killed its two Division commanders, and Van Dorn had given Price orders to get out the best way he could, which forced him to retreat to the east towards White River.

After the Pea Ridge campaign the Battle of Prairie Grove was fought, under the command of General F. C. Herring, who was Lieutenant-Colonel of the Ninth Iowa Infantry in the Battle of Pea Ridge. As it was not in my command I have no knowledge of the detail of it; but from the reports it evidently was a sharp fight.

In the spring of 1865 Jeff C. Thompson and his command surrendered to me on the Arkansas line. His command consisted of six thousand men, but he found he could not gather them, and claimed that not half of his command was present. When I asked him how it was possible to get them all together, he suggested that I should send them rations. I therefore loaded two steamers from St. Louis, and sent them around by the White River, and Thompson issued his celebrated order bringing the men all in, and there was gathered about twice the number he had present when he surrendered to my forces. When asked for his transportation he said that he would show it to me, and out of the rivers and bayous he run down about one hundred canoes and flats, as the transportation he had to move his army with. It was at this time that he made that celebrated speech. When his soldiers came in without bringing their guns, as he had instructed them to do, bringing along old shot-guns and muskets that were of no use, he said if they were not satisfied with the generosity of this Government they should emigrate to Mexico, and he denounced more than half of them as being [Pg 142] soldiers whom he had never seen, stating that they had stayed in the brush and along the river-banks in Arkansas until the moss had grown upon their heads and backs. From this speech of his came the celebrated saying of "moss-backs."

A part of my Corps fought under that gallant General, A. J. Smith, in the Banks campaign up the Red River, and there is no doubt but that his generalship and the fighting of the two Divisions of the Sixteenth Corps saved that Army from a great defeat. The commander of one of his Divisions, General T. E. G. Ransom, was a schoolmate of mine, and afterwards came to me in the Atlanta campaign and commanded a Division under me in the Sixteenth Corps.

When I look at the history of all of the operations west of the Mississippi River, and see their results, it is a great gratification to me to know that all the campaigns, except possibly the one of Banks, were victories for our side.

When I returned to the command of the Department of the Missouri, in November, 1864, I found all the Indian tribes on the plains at war, occupying all the lines of communication through to the Pacific, and there was a great demand from the people upon the Government that those lines should be opened. General Grant sent a dispatch, asking if a campaign upon the plains could be made in the winter. Having spent eight or ten years of my life upon the plains before the war, I answered that it could, if the troops were properly fed and clothed. His answer to that was to place all the plains and Indian tribes within my command, instructing me to make an immediate campaign against them, and I had, therefore, to move the troops that were at Leavenworth, Fort Riley, and other points, onto the plains in mid-winter, and I think it was the Eleventh Kansas that had thirteen men frozen to death on the march to Fort Kearney. Those troops on that winter march up and down those stage- and telegraph-lines, in forty days opened them up, repaired the telegraph, and had the stages running. Then came the longer campaign of the next summer and next fall, where General Cole's command suffered so much, and also where General Conner fought the Battle of Tongue River. I remember of the Indians capturing a company of Michigan troops that were guarding a train that was going to Fort Halleck, loaded with rations and bacon. They tied some of the soldiers to the wheels of the wagons, piled the bacon around the wagons, and burned them up. A band of this [Pg

143] party of Indians was captured by a battalion of Pawnees, who were far north of them and got on their trail and surrounded the band that had committed these atrocities. The chief of them, an old man, came forward and spoke to Major North, who commanded the Pawnees, and holding his hand up to his mouth he said that he was full of white men up to here, and was ready to die. The Indians virtually cleaned out the white people along the stage-lines they captured. I took from them a great many of their prisoners in the fall of 1865, when they came into Laramie to make peace, and the stories of the suffering of the women were such that it would be impossible to relate them.

In connection with this campaign on the plains, it is a singular fact that nearly three thousand Confederates took part. When I took command at St. Louis I found the prisons full of Confederate prisoners. The war was then virtually at its end, and they were very anxious to be relieved from prison life, and as we needed forces on the plains, I obtained authority from the War Department to organize what was known as the United States Volunteers, and filled the regiments with these Confederate soldiers, placing over them as officers, men and officers selected from our own command, and thus organized a very effective force, which did excellent service on the plains, three-quarters of which remained in that country after the war was over.

[Pg 144]

Place on the Battlefield of Atlanta, on the right of the battle line of the Sixteenth Army Corps, where Major-General James B. McPherson, commanding the Army of the Tennessee, was killed, July 22, 1864. The wheels are portions of Murray's Second U. S. Battery, which was captured by the Confederate skirmish-line while passing from the Seventeenth to the Sixteenth Corps.

[Pg 145]

A TALK TO OLD COMRADES

Address to Sixteenth Army Corps
Delivered at the National Encampment, G. A. R.
Washington, D. C., October, 1902
By Major-General Grenville M. Dodge

Comrades of the Sixteenth Army Corps:

The Sixteenth Army Corps was organized December 18th, 1862, and formed into two wings. General A. J. Smith commanded the right wing, and General G. M. Dodge the left wing of the Corps. The left wing was organized with the Corps, the right wing a year or more afterwards. The Corps, as a body, was never together, though it probably took part in more widely separated fields than any other Corps in the Army of the Tennessee. The right wing, under General Smith, was in the Vicksburg campaign, and after that it went to the Department of the Gulf, and was with General Banks in his movement up Red River, and saved that Army from defeat; of this there is no doubt. After that, it was sent after Forrest, and it was the only command that I know of that caught and whipped him. The left wing overtook General Forrest at Town Creek, in 1863, in its march to Decatur in the rear of Bragg's Army, but he did not stay long enough for us to get a good fight out of him.

From the campaign after Forrest, General Smith's command was sent to the Department of the Missouri to drive out Price. There I found them, in December, 1864, when I took command of that Department, in a deplorable condition,—without clothing, shoes, or camp equipage. Under an order from General Grant, I sent them to Nashville, with all the force in my department, some twenty thousand men all told, to help General Thomas, and I sent them everything they needed to clothe and equip them. You all remember how you were frozen in on the Mississippi, and had to take the cars. One of the pleasantest recollections of my life is [Pg 146] that I received a letter from General Smith, thanking me for appreciating their condition, and having in Nashville when they arrived, everything they needed. He said that it was the first time they had been treated decently, and they were thankful they had fallen into the hands of some one who appreciated them.

At the Battle of Nashville it was General Smith, with the right wing of the Sixteenth Corps, and the troops of the Department of the Missouri, that turned the left flank of Hood's Army, and was practically in his rear when stopped; and I have heard many officers who were there say that if he had been let alone he would have captured or destroyed that wing of the Army. Thus ended the eventful career of the right wing, and its fortunes were cast with the Army of the Cumberland in its chase after Hood.

The left wing was organized from the troops I commanded in the District of Corinth, and had in it the old Second Division of the Army of the Tennessee that Grant organized at Cairo, that fought at Belmont, Henry and Donelson, Shiloh, and the two Corinths. It had on its banners, "First at Donelson." I took command right after the Battle of Corinth, where it had been censured by Rosecrans and praised by Grant for the part it took in the Battle of Corinth. General Grant held us at Corinth as a protection to his communications while the campaign against Vicksburg was going on. In a letter to me he said he had left us there to protect that flank, for he knew that if Bragg endeavored to break that line we would stay; so you see he still had faith in his old Division. From Corinth we marched with

Sherman in his celebrated trip from Memphis to Chattanooga. We wintered on the line, and rebuilt the Nashville and Decatur Road, and in his Memoirs General Grant, after describing the condition of the Army, and the necessity for rebuilding the railway from Nashville to Decatur, speaks thus of the work of the Sixteenth Army Corps:

General Dodge had no tools to work with except those of the pioneer — axes, picks, and spades. With these he was enabled to intrench his men, and protect them against surprise from small parties of the enemy, and, as he had no base of supplies until the road could be completed back to Nashville, the first matter to consider, after protecting his men, was the getting in of food and forage from the surrounding country. He had his men and teams bring in all the grain they could find, or all they needed, and all the cattle for beef, and such other food as could be found. Millers were detailed from the ranks to run the mills along the line of the army. Where they were not near enough to the troops for protection they were taken down and moved up to the line of the road. Blacksmith shops, with all the iron and steel found in them, were used up in like manner. Blacksmiths [Pg 147] were detailed and set to work making the tools necessary in railroad and bridge building. Axemen were at work getting out timber for bridges, and cutting fuel for locomotives and cars. Thus every branch of railroad building, making tools to work with, and supplying the workmen with food, was all going on at once, and without the aid of a mechanic or workman except what the command itself furnished. General Dodge had the work assigned to him finished within forty days after receiving his orders. The number of bridges to rebuild was 182, many of them over deep and wide chasms. The length of road repaired was 102 miles.

I only quote a small part of what General Grant says in this connection, to show you that while the Sixteenth Corps had its share of fighting, and praise for it, still it was a Corps that Grant called upon in an emergency, and when he wanted great deeds done; and proves not only what they could turn their hands to when necessary, but is also a sample of what our great army was made of.

In the spring of 1864 we became a part of the great Army in the Atlanta campaign. When we arrived at Chattanooga, on the 5th of May, I called at General Sherman's headquarters. General McPherson, our Army Commander, was there. Sherman said to him: "You had better send Dodge to take Ship's Gap." "Why, General," replied McPherson, "that is thirty miles away, and Dodge's troops are not yet unloaded, and he has no transportation with him." Sherman said: "Let him try it, and have the transportation follow." We struck out, and that night at midnight Sprague's Brigade of the Fourth Division of the Sixteenth Corps had gained the Gap. The enemy appeared the next morning. This opened the way through Snake Creek Gap, planting us in the rear of Johnston's Army, and forcing him to abandon his impregnable position at Dalton.

Our battles in the Atlanta campaign were those of the Army of the Tennessee. The left wing received continual commendation until the great battle of the 22d, when it happened to be in the rear of our Army, and received and defeated the celebrated movement of Hood to our rear. Sprague's Brigade fought all day at Decatur, and saved our trains. In the battle of the 22d of July we had only five thousand men in line, but met and repulsed three Divisions of Hardee's Corps, and McPherson, who stood on our right and witnessed the fight, watching the charge of Fuller and Mersey, and the breaking of two of the enemy's columns, spoke of us in the highest terms, and five minutes later was dead. Our Army, who knew and loved him, never could reconcile ourselves to his great loss.

[Pg 148] The Battle of Atlanta was one of the few battles of the war where the attack on the Sixteenth Army Corps caught it on the march in the rear of the Army, without intrenchments or protection of any kind, both sides fighting in the open.

In his address describing the battle of the 22d of July, General Strong, of General McPherson's staff, says:

General McPherson and myself, accompanied only by our orderlies, rode out and took position on the right of Dodge's line, and witnessed the desperate assaults of Hood's army. General McPherson's admiration for the steadiness and bravery of the Sixteenth Corps was unbounded. Had the Sixteenth Corps given way the rebel army would have been in the rear of the Seventeenth and Fifteenth Corps, and would have swept like an avalanche over our supply-trains, and the position of the Army of the Tennessee would have been very critical.

General Frank P. Blair pays this tribute to the fighting of the Sixteenth Army Corps, in his official report of the Battle of Atlanta:

I started to go back to my command, and witnessed the fearful assault made on the Sixteenth Army Corps, and its prompt and gallant repulse by that command. It was a most fortunate circumstance for the whole army that the Sixteenth Army Corps occupied the position I have attempted to describe at the moment of attack; and, although it does not belong to me to report upon the bearing and conduct of the officers and men of that Corps, still I cannot withhold my expression of admiration for the manner in which this command met and repulsed the repeated and persistent attacks of the enemy. The attack upon our flank and rear was made by the whole of Hardee's corps.

Under General Howard, a part of the left wing took part in the battle of the 28th of July. On August 19th I was given a Confederate leave, when that *beau-ideal* of a soldier, my old schoolmate and comrade, General T. E. G. Ransom, took command of the Corps. The right wing knew him, for he was with you in the Red River campaign. He died on a stretcher in command of the Corps in the chase after Hood. The old Second Division had its innings with General Corse, at Altoona, where the fighting has been immortalized in verse and song. My fortunes took me away to the command of the Army and Department of the Missouri, and the two Divisions of the left wing were merged one into the Fifteenth and the other into the Seventeenth Corps, and, so far as the campaigns were concerned, the Corps fought in two units, the right and left wings, and each was a Corps command.

The grave of that remarkable soldier, General A. J. Smith, whose distinguished services were so often recognized by Generals Grant and Sherman, has not a stone to designate it. The Society [Pg 149] of the Army of the Tennessee is aiding in raising the funds to commemorate his memory and deeds by erecting a monument in his home in St. Louis.

The Sixteenth Army Corps had great opportunities in the campaigns it took part in, and never failed to make the most of them. They went cheerfully to any work assigned to them. They have left in the war records a history that they may well be proud of, and every work they have undertaken has received the strong commendation of their superior officers.

[Pg 150]

MAJOR-GENERAL GEORGE G. MEADE

Commander
Army of the Potomac
1864

[Pg 151]

GENERAL GRANT

Remarks at Army of Potomac Reunion
Niagara Falls, N. Y.

When you consider that it is now thirty-three years after the war, that the Government has published every report, letter and order that was of any moment, you will agree with me that it is difficult to interest an Army audience in talking about another Army, and I shall not detain you long on that subject. There are, however, some incidents of General Grant's first visit to your Army, his return to ours, and the planning of the grand campaign that was to end the war, that may interest you.

In December, 1863, after the Battle of Chattanooga, the Army of the Tennessee camped along the railway from Columbia, Tenn., to Decatur and Huntsville, Ala. After the Battle of Chattanooga General Grant returned to Nashville and called there to meet him several Corps Commanders of the Army of the Tennessee, and General Sheridan of the Army of the Cumberland. If I remember rightly, there were present Generals Grant, Sherman, Sheridan, Granger, Logan, Rawlins, and myself. All of us of the Army of the Tennessee were a hard-looking crowd. None of us had seen Nashville or any base of supplies since we had marched from the Mississippi River to Chattanooga, and we had been hard at work building railways and foraging. We arrived in Nashville late in the afternoon, and General Sherman took us to General Grant's headquarters. General Grant suggested that we should call upon the Military Governor of Tennessee, Andrew Johnson, and pay our respects to him. We, of course, followed General Grant, and were introduced to Governor Johnson. I remember that our uniforms were greatly worn, one or two of us wearing blouses with Army overcoats, and he looked at us with a very quizzical eye, until General Grant said to excuse us that he had not given us time since we reached the city to change our suits; but Grant knew we had no [Pg 152] others. Governor Johnson was then a very radical man, and was very emphatic in informing us that while he was Military Governor of Tennessee no rebel would receive much consideration from him, and brought his fist down on a piano in the room with such force that the sound from it startled us all, and we left there with the idea that rebels in Tennessee had better get out; but we soon found that his words were much stronger than his acts, for I hardly ever got my hands on rebel stock or supplies that I did not find Johnson trying to pull them off.

After our visit, General Sherman suggested that we should all go to the theater that evening, and under his lead we went to the principal opera house to hear the play of Hamlet. We were all strangers in Nashville; even General Grant was not well known. We paid our way in and found the theater crowded with soldiers going to and returning from veteran furloughs. General Sherman, who you all know was a great lover of the theater, sat alongside of me and soon commenced criticising the play, earnestly protesting that it was being murdered. I had to check him several times and tell him unless he kept quiet the soldiers in the audience would recognize him and there would be a scene. We had entered late, and there soon came on the scene where Hamlet soliloquizes over the skull of Yorick. The audience was perfectly still, endeavoring to comprehend the actor's words, when a soldier far back in the audience rose up and in a clear voice called out, as the actor held up the skull, "Say, pard, what is it, Yank or Reb?" The house appreciated the point and was instantly in an uproar, and General Grant said we had better leave, so we went quietly out, no one discovering Grant's or Sherman's presence. Sherman immediately suggested that we should find an oyster-house and get something to eat, and General Rawlins was put forward as guide and spokesman. He led us to a very inviting place. We went in and found there was but one large table in the place. There was one man sitting at it, and Rawlins, in his modest way, without informing the man who his party was, asked him if he would change to a smaller table and let us have that one. The man said the table was good enough for him and kept on eating, and Rawlins backed out into the street again. Sherman said if we depended on Rawlins we would get nothing to eat, and said he would see what could be done. He hailed a man who pointed out another saloon kept by a woman, and to this Sherman took us, and she served us what we then [Pg 153] considered a very nice oyster stew. As we sat around the table, we talked more than we ate, and by the time we had half finished our supper the woman came in

172

and asked for the pay and said we must leave, as under the military rules her house must close at 12 midnight and it was then a few minutes after that hour; so out we got and took our way to Grant's headquarters, where we bunked down the best we could during the night. Some of the staff heard of our evening's adventure and gave the news to the press, and the next morning before breakfast all the parties were present to apologize to Grant that they did not recognize him, as we were out of our own jurisdiction and in that of the Army of the Cumberland; but Grant in his modest way satisfied them that he had no complaint. However, there poured in on him for all of us complimentary tickets and invitations to almost everything in Nashville.

After breakfast we all assembled in a large room at headquarters to hear what General Grant had to say to us. He took up with us the plan for a winter campaign. He proposed himself to take about 30,000 of the troops concentrated at Chattanooga and transport them by the Ohio and Mississippi Rivers to New Orleans, and there take with him the troops of General Canby and go thence to Mobile and attack that place. General Sherman was to go to Memphis, gather up all the forces along the Mississippi River, including the troops at Vicksburg and Natchez, together with the Seventeenth Corps, and march from Vicksburg to Meridian and thence join Grant at Mobile. I was to take the Sixteenth Corps, which was then located on the line of the Nashville and Decatur road, together with about 10,000 cavalry that General William Sooy Smith had concentrated near Nashville, and sweep down through Alabama, Northern Mississippi, and Western Tennessee, attacking any forces of the enemy that might be met, and destroying all the railroads and provisions that had been stored in that country, this with a view of making it difficult for any of the confederate armies to again occupy the territory, so as to enable Sherman and Grant, when the spring and summer campaign came on, to utilize all the Union troops that had been occupying that country. After the plans were all made and all the arrangements agreed upon, General Grant reported them to Washington, but President Lincoln objected because he was afraid, if we took so many troops from Chattanooga, that Longstreet, who was occupying Eastern Tennessee with his Army, would return to Chattanooga or Middle Tennessee [Pg 154] and undo all we had accomplished in the Battle of Chattanooga. Grant had no fear of this, but he made up his mind to go immediately to East Tennessee and take the forces there under General Foster, attack and defeat Longstreet, and then come back and carry out his plans. He found after reaching Knoxville that General Foster's forces could not be used, so he abandoned the campaign, only sending Sherman to Vicksburg, who marched out to Meridian and returned, while the 7,000 cavalry under General William Sooy Smith, who was to join Sherman overland, moved south, fighting and driving the enemy until he reached West Point, where he met a superior force of the enemy and returned to Memphis.

In March, 1864, General Grant was called to Washington to be given his commission as Lieutenant-General of the Army and command of all the forces. On his return to Nashville, on March 17th, we were again called to meet him. General Grant told us of his visit to Washington, his reception by the President, and all the courtesies that had been paid him. He told us that he accepted the commission of Lieutenant-General and Commander of all the Armies on condition that his plans should not be interfered with at Washington and that he should have the command of the staff departments of the armies. Those departments had always considered themselves independent of the Commander in the field; in fact, in the beginning of the war the officers of Commissary Quarter-Master and Ordnance Departments declined to obey the orders of the commanders they were serving under, except upon the order of their chief in Washington. General Grant settled this. A Commissary of Subsistence declined to carry out one of his orders, and General Grant said to him that while he could not force him to obey the order, he could relieve him and put in his place one of the line officers who would obey all orders. This officer reported this to Washington and it changed their orders so that they were ordered to obey the orders of the officer in the field and to report their orders to their chiefs in Washington. General Grant said that President Lincoln said in reply to his request for the command of the staff departments that he could not give him that legally; but, he said, "There is no one but myself that can interfere with your orders; and you can rest assured that I will not do it." We were all anxious to hear of his visit to the Army of the Potomac, and his opinion of it, and Sherman soon got him to talking about it. [Pg 155] He said it was the finest Army he had ever seen; far superior to any of ours in equipment, supplies, and transportation. He said, however, that the officers he talked with considered he would have a much more difficult problem on his hands than he had had in the West, and he said to Sherman that some officer who both of them knew, but whose name I have forgotten, told him, "You have not faced Bobby Lee yet;" and as he said it, I could see that twinkle in Grant's eye that we often saw there when he meant mischief. Grant, after discussing the Army of the Potomac and having nothing but praise for it, informed us that he should make his headquarters with that Army and leave Sherman to command the Armies of the West, also informing us that he proposed to take several of us East with him. Sherman protested strongly against this, and it was finally compromised by his taking Sheridan and leaving the rest of us with Sherman. During the two or three days we were with Grant he outlined in a general way his plan of campaign that every Army should move as early as possible in the spring, all on the same day against the enemy, so that Lee and Johnston could not detach any of their commands to reinforce the others. He said, "I will try to keep Lee from sending any force to Johnston, but," he said to Sherman, "if he does, I will send you two men where he sends one." He also informed us of the necessity of closing the war with this campaign.

Our visit with Grant ended, he took Sherman as far as Cincinnati with him, to talk over and complete their plans, while we returned to our commands to fit them out for the campaign. General Sherman has since pointed out to me in the Burnett House, at Cincinnati, the room they occupied the night before they parted, and where over their maps the final orders were given him and final arrangements made that inaugurated the two great campaigns of Richmond and Petersburg in the East, and Atlanta in the West. After the Atlanta campaign I paid General Grant a visit at City Point. I reached his headquarters in October, and spent two weeks with him, and saw the Armies of the James and the Potomac. Evenings we would sit around his camp-fire, and in his genial, comprehensive way, he told us of his campaign and the great battles you had fought, and brought out fully to me what a great Army you were. I asked him what he claimed for the Battle of the Wilderness. There had been great discussion, as you know, about it, and Grant, with the same twinkle of the eye that I had seen at [Pg 156] Nashville, said, "I only claim that after that battle, (and I took the initiative on the march towards Richmond,) that the Army of the Potomac was no longer afraid of Bobby Lee." He had not forgotten his talk with us at Nashville.

Now you have had Grant's opinion of your great Army, and as my toast is the Army of the Tennessee, I will close by giving you General Grant's description of that Army when called upon to respond to the same toast at one of our reunions. He said, "As an Army, the Army of the Tennessee never sustained a single defeat during four years of war. Every fortification which it assailed surrendered. Every force arrayed against it was either defeated, captured, or destroyed. No officer was ever assigned to the command of that army who had afterwards to be relieved from it or to be reduced to another command. Such a history is not accident."

[Pg 157]

[Pg 158]

176

PONTOON BRIDGE ACROSS THE TENNESSEE RIVER AT DECATUR, ALA.

Built by the Sixteenth Army Corps in the spring of 1864, Major-General G. M. Dodge commanding. Copy of painting made at the time by an enlisted man and presented to General Dodge.

[Pg 159]

USE OF BLOCK-HOUSES DURING THE CIVIL WAR

To the Editor of the Army and Navy Journal:

I was greatly interested in the communication of Captain Joubert Reitz, published in your journal March 21, 1903, giving a description of the block-house system inaugurated by General Kitchener in the Transvaal War. It was a continuous line of block-houses connected by barbed wire, to prevent the Boers crossing the railway lines, and virtually corralling their forces in certain districts until want of food forced them to surrender. Captain Reitz asserts that the block-house system did more to end the war than the whole British Army.

In the Civil War our block-house system was just as effective, but in another direction. We used it for the purpose of protecting our lines of communication, not as a trocha, or a line connected with wire fencing and other obstructions, as used by the British and by the Spaniards in the Cuban War. The British built theirs of bags filled with earth. The Spaniards erected neat structures of two stories, built of concrete, with wooden roofs and openings for two lines of fire, one above the other. These were erected not more than half a mile apart. In the Civil War our block-houses were usually erected of logs, one and two stories high. The face of the upper story had an angle of forty-five degrees to the face of the first story, thus concentrating a direct fire upon an enemy approaching from any point of the compass. The first block-houses in the West that I know of were built by my command in July and August, 1862, when it re-built the Mobile & Ohio Railroad from Columbus to Humbolt. There were many important bridges on this line, and we built block-houses at the most important ones, and stockades at the others.

In the fall of 1862, when Forrest and Jackson made the noted raids into West Tennessee, the forces at all these structures that my command had erected held their positions, and defeated the [Pg 160] enemy when attacked, while at the bridges between Jackson, Tennessee, and Grand Junction, where they had only earth defenses, the forces were driven away or captured and the bridges destroyed. The result of this was that General Grant issued an order commending the action of the detachments that were successful, stating that wherever they stood success followed, and the enemy suffered a loss in killed and wounded greater than the garrisons of the block-houses and stockades. This result also caused General Grant to issue an order to build block-houses and stockades on the line of the Memphis & Charleston Railway at all important bridges from Memphis to Corinth, and they protected this line of communication until it was abandoned.

The block-houses held about a company, but sometimes stockades or earth intrenchments were added to hold two companies, and our orders were imperative to all forces occupying them never to leave them or surrender, no matter how large the attacking force. My first order stated that a company in a block-house or stockade was equal to a Regiment attacking, and I do not remember the enemy, in their numerous raids, ever capturing one that was defended, up to the time I left Corinth in the summer of 1863. After the Battle of Chattanooga, when our Armies were lying along the line of the railway from Nashville to Decatur and Nashville to Stevenson, I rebuilt the Nashville & Decatur Railway, on which there were at least thirty important bridges, at each of which we built strong block-houses and stockades, and the enemy never captured one of them, though in two instances they were attacked with a brigade, and often with two Regiments and batteries. We protected against artillery fire by throwing up earthworks to the height of the first line of fire, taking the chance of any damage being done above that. Our orders here were when Forest, Roddy, and Hannan attacked this line to hold the posts under any and all circumstances, stating that if they stayed in the block-houses and stockades nothing could defeat them, and so it proved. Where these forces struck a Regiment, and captured it in earth-works, they went twelve miles north to the Sulphur Trestle, a bridge one hundred and twenty-five feet high, defended by two companies in a block-house and stockade, and were signally defeated. The Army of the Cumberland protected the line from Nashville to Stevenson, and on to Chattanooga, with block-houses at all bridges and important points, and when on the 5th of May, 1864, General Sherman [Pg 161] started on the Atlanta campaign, General Hooker reports on April 23, 1864, that he detailed 1,460 men to occupy block-houses from Nashville to Chattanooga, and this force held that line of road throughout the campaign, though many attempts were made to destroy it. During the Atlanta campaign as we advanced the railway was rebuilt, and all bridges and stations had block-houses or stockades to protect them.

General Green B. Raum's Brigade was located at some of the most important structures. General Wheeler, with all of Johnston's Cavalry force and several batteries, endeavored to destroy this, our only line of communication for transporting supplies. General Raum's story is so to the point that I quote it almost entire. He says:

My experiences with block-houses extended from May to November, 1864, on the Memphis & Charleston railroad, and the Chattanooga & Atlanta railroad. Block-houses were built along these railroads exclusively for the protection of bridges. They were built of heavy square timbers, sometimes with two or three thicknesses of timber, and were of various sizes. I had a two-story block-house built at Mud Creek, east of Scottsboro, Ala.; it would easily hold 100 men. These houses were carefully pierced with loop-holes, so that the garrison could cover every approach. My garrisons were usually too large for the block-houses. In these cases I threw up an earth-work, and protected it with abatis. The Confederate forces soon learned to respect a block-house. I found it to be an absolute defense against musketry.

During the Atlanta campaign our block-houses were constantly attacked by raiding parties; small and great trains would be thrown from the track and burned, and small sections of the track destroyed. About July 5, 1864, an enterprising Confederate cavalryman with about 300 men made a rapid march up Dirt Town Valley, crossed the Chattanooga range by a bridle-path, threw a train of fifteen loaded cars off the track, burned them, and destroyed a small section of the track, but he did not attempt to destroy the bridge near by at Tilton — it was defended by a block-house with a capacity for seventy men.

When General Wheeler made his great raid north in August, 1864, he struck the railroad at various places. He destroyed two miles of track immediately south of Tilton, Ga., but did not come within range of the block-house, and did not attempt to destroy the bridge defended by the block-house. During this raid General Wheeler, without hesitation, attacked and carried a part of the works at Dalton. During the Atlanta campaign there was not a bridge destroyed by the Confederates between Nashville and Atlanta which was protected by a block-house.

After the fall of Atlanta, General Hood moved with his entire army against the Chattanooga and Atlanta railroad, destroying thirty-seven miles of track. On October 12 he struck the railroad at Resaca and Tilton. Tilton was garrisoned by the Seventeenth Iowa. Lieutenant-Colonel Archer commanding. He had about 350 men — no artillery. An Army Corps was in his front. Colonel Archer held the enemy off seven hours, fighting from his rifle-pits and block-house. At last the Confederate commander placed several batteries in position, and opened upon the devoted garrison. In a short time the block-house was rendered untenable, and Colonel Archer was forced to surrender. This was the first and only success against our block-house system. On December 4, 1814, Bates's division of Cheatham's Corps attacked the block-house at the railroad crossing of Overall's Creek, five miles [Pg 162] north of Murfreesborough, Tenn. The enemy used artillery to reduce the block-house, and although seventy-four shots were fired at it, no material injury was done; the garrison held out until relieved by General Milroy from Murfreesborough.

After the Atlanta campaign, in the Department of the Missouri, every important bridge and town where detachments of troops were stationed was protected by block-houses and stockades, and during the Indian campaigns of 1864-5-6 our lines of communication, stage and telegraph, were all held successfully by small detachments of troops in block-houses and stockades, and were never captured unless overwhelming forces of the Indians attacked them, and only then when the defensive works were inferior or not properly constructed; and, even in cases where detachments left their stations, if they had remained they would have successfully held them. After I took command on the plains and issued positive orders for detachments to stay by their posts and never leave them, not a single detachment that I remember of was captured in its block-house or stockade. With the small force we had it would have been impossible to maintain our mail, telegraph and overland routes successfully, if it had not been for our system of block-houses and stockades, dotted for thousands of miles over each of the overland routes. It is evident from our experience in the West that our block-house and stockade system of defending our lines of communication was a great success, not only as against raids of cavalry, but from attacks of infantry and artillery, and saved to us a very large force for the field. I left on the line of the railway from Nashville to Athens during the Atlanta campaign only two Regiments of negroes, taking with me my entire Corps, and without the block-houses to defend the lines from Nashville to Stevenson and Stevenson to Atlanta, it would have taken a thousand men without block-house protection for every hundred required with it.

Grenville M. Dodge.

[Pg 163]

[Pg 164]

Monument erected in Nashville, Tenn., to Samuel Davis, Confederate Spy executed by order of General Dodge, at Pulaski, Tenn., in 1864.

[Pg 165]

AN INCIDENT OF THE WAR

Execution of the Confederate Spy, Samuel Davis
at Pulaski, Tenn., November, 1863

New York, June 15th, 1897.

To the Editor of The Confederate Veteran:

In fulfillment of my promise to give you my recollections of Sam Davis, (who was hung as a spy in November, 1863, at Pulaski, Tenn.,) I desire to say that in writing of matters which occurred thirty-four years ago one is apt to make mistakes as to minor details; but the principal facts were such that they impressed themselves upon my mind so that I can speak of them with some certainty.

When General Grant ordered General Sherman (whose head of column was near Eastport, on the Tennessee River) to drop everything and bring his army to Chattanooga, my Corps (the Sixteenth) was then located at Corinth, Miss., and I brought up the rear.

General Grant's anxiety to attack Bragg's command before Longstreet could return from East Tennessee brought on the battle before I could reach Chattanooga. General Grant, therefore, instructed General Sherman to halt my command in Middle Tennessee and to instruct me to rebuild the railway from Nashville to Decatur. The fulfilling of the above order is fully set forth by General Grant in his Memoirs.

When I reached the line of the Nashville and Decatur railroad, I distributed my troops from Columbia south towards Athens, Alabama. I had about 10,000 men and 8,000 animals, and was without provisions, with no railroad or water communication to any base of supply, and was obliged to draw subsistence for my command from the adjacent country until I could rebuild the railroad and receive my supplies from Nashville.

My command was a part of the Army of the Tennessee, occupying [Pg 166] temporarily a portion of the territory of the Department of the Cumberland, but not reporting or subject to the commander of that department.

Upon an examination of the country, I found that there was an abundance of everything needed to supply my command, except where Sherman's forces had swept across it along Elk River. He wrote me, "I do not think that my forces have left a chicken for you." I also found that I was in a country where the sentiment of the people was almost unanimously against us. I had very little faith in converting them by the taking of the oath of allegiance; I therefore issued an order stating that I required the products of the country to supply my command, and that to all who had these products, regardless of their sentiments, who would bring them to the stations where my troops were located, I would pay a fair price for them; but that, if I had to send and bring the supplies myself, I should take them without making payment, giving them only receipts; and also issued instructions that every train going for supplies should be accompanied by an officer and receipt given for what he took. This had a good effect, the citizens generally bringing in their supplies to my command and receiving the proper voucher; but it also gave an opportunity for straggling bands to rob and charge up their depredations to my command. This caused many complaints to be filed with the military governor of Tennessee and the Department Commander of the Army of the Cumberland.

Upon investigation I found most of those depredations were committed by irresponsible parties of both sides, and I also discovered that there was a well-organized and disciplined Corps of scouts and spies within my lines, one force operating to the east of the line, under Captain Coleman, and another force operating to the west, having its headquarters in the vicinity of Florence, Alabama. I issued orders to my own spies to locate these parties, sending out scouting parties to wipe them out or drive them across the Tennessee River.

My cavalry had had considerable experience in this work in and around Corinth, and they were very successful and brought in many prisoners, most of whom could only be treated as prisoners of war.

The Seventh Kansas Cavalry was very efficient in this service, and they captured Samuel Davis, Joshua Brown, Smith, and [Pg 167] General Bragg's Chief of Scouts and Secret Service Colonel S. Shaw, all about the same time. We did not know of the importance of the capture of Shaw, or that he was the Captain Coleman commanding Bragg's secret-service force. Nothing was found on any of the prisoners of importance, except upon Davis, who evidently had been selected to carry the information they had all obtained through to General Bragg. Upon Davis were found letters from Captain Coleman, the commander of the scouts to the east of us, and many others. I was very anxious to capture Coleman and break up his command, as my own scouts and spies within the Confederate lines were continually reporting to us the news sent south from and the movements of Coleman within my lines.

Davis was brought immediately to me, as his captors knew his importance. They believed he was an officer and also knew he was a member of Coleman's command.

When brought to my office I met him pleasantly. I knew what had been found upon him and I desired to locate Coleman and his command and ascertain, if possible, who was furnishing the information, which I saw was accurate and valuable, to General Bragg.

Davis met me modestly. He was a fine, soldierly-looking young man, dressed in a faded Federal soldier's coat, one of our army soft hats, and top boots. He had a frank, open face, which was inclined to brightness. I tried to impress upon him the danger he was in, and that I knew he was only a messenger, and held out to him the hope of lenient treatment if he would answer truthfully, as far as he could, my questions.

He listened attentively and respectfully to me, but, as I recollect, made no definite answer, and I had him returned to the prison. My recollection is that Captain Armstrong, my Provost Marshal, placed in the prison with him and the other prisoners one of our own spies, who claimed to them to be one of the Confederate scouting parties operating within my lines, and I think the man More, whom the other prisoners speak of as having been captured with them and escaping, was this man. However, they all kept their own counsel and we obtained no information of value from them.

The reason of this reticence was the fact that they all knew Colonel Shaw was one of our captives, and that if his importance [Pg 168] was made known to us he would certainly be hung; and they did not think that Davis would be executed.

Upon Davis was found a large mail of value. Much of it was letters from the friends and relatives of soldiers in the Confederate Army. There were many small presents — one or two, I remember, to General Bragg — and much accurate information of my forces, of our defenses, our intentions, substance of my orders, criticisms as to my treatment of the citizens, and a general approval of my payment for supplies, while a few denounced severely some of the parties who had hauled in supplies under the orders. Captain Coleman mentioned this in one of his letters.

There were also intimations of the endeavor that would be made to interrupt my work, and plans for the capture of single soldiers and small parties of the command out after forage.

I had Davis brought before me again, after my Provost Marshal had reported his inability to obtain anything of value from him. I then informed him that he would be tried as a spy; that the evidence against him would surely convict him; and made a direct appeal to him to give me the information I knew he had. He very quietly, but firmly, refused to do it. I therefore let him be tried and suffer the consequences. Considerable interest was taken in young Davis by the Provost Marshal and Chaplain Young, and considerable pressure was brought to bear upon them by some of the citizens of Pulaski; and I am under the impression that some of them saw Davis and endeavored to induce him to save himself, but they failed. Mrs. John A. Jackson, I remember, made a personal appeal in his behalf directly to me. Davis was convicted upon trial and sentenced. Then one of my noted scouts, known as "Chickasaw," believed that he could prevail upon Davis to give the information we asked.

He took him in hand and never gave it up until the last moment, going to the scaffold with a promise of pardon a few moments before his execution.

Davis died to save his own chief, Colonel Shaw, who was in prison with him and was captured the same day.

The parties who were prisoners with Davis have informed me that it was Shaw who had selected Davis as the messenger to General Bragg, and had given to him part of his mail and papers.

I did not know this certainly until a long time after the war. I first learned of it by rumor and what some of my own scouts have [Pg 169] told me since the war, and it has since been confirmed confidentially to me by one of the prisoners who was captured about the same time that Davis was and who was imprisoned with him up to the time he was convicted and sentenced, and knew Colonel Shaw, as well as all the facts in the case.

The statement made to me is, that Colonel S. Shaw was the chief or an important officer in General Bragg's Secret-Service Corps; that Shaw had furnished the important documents to Davis; and that their captors did not know Shaw and his importance.

Colonel Shaw I sent with the other prisoners North, as prisoners of war. I also learned that Shaw was greatly alarmed when he was informed I was trying to induce Davis to give me the information he had.

This is where Davis showed himself a true soldier. He had been entrusted with an important commission by an important officer, who was imprisoned with him, and died rather than betray him. He knew to a certainty, if he informed me of the facts, that Shaw would be executed, for he was a far more important person to us than was Davis.

During the war I had many spies captured; some executed who were captured within the Confederate lines and who were equally brave in meeting their fate.

By an extraordinary effort I saved the life of one who was captured by Forrest. Through my efforts this man escaped, though General Forrest sized him up correctly. He was one of the most important men we ever had within the Confederate lines.

Forrest was determined to hang him, but Major-General Polk believed him innocent and desired to save him.

Great interest was taken in Davis at the time, because it was known by all of the command that I desired to save him.

Your publication bears many evidences of this fact. It is not, therefore, necessary for me to state that I regretted to see sentence executed; but it was one of the fates of war, which is cruelty itself, and there is no refining it.

I find this letter bearing upon the case; it may be of interest. It is my first report to Major B. M. Sawyer, Assistant Adjutant-General, Army of the Tennessee, notifying him of the capture of Davis. It is dated, Pulaski, Tenn., November 20th, 1863, and is as follows:

[Pg 170] I herewith inclose a copy of dispatches taken from one of Bragg's spies. He had a heavy mail, papers, etc., and shows Captain Coleman is pretty well posted.

We have broken up several bands of mounted robbers and Confederate cavalry in the last week, capturing some five commissioned officers and one hundred enlisted men, who have been forwarded.

I also forward a few of the most important letters found in the mail. The tooth-brushes and blank-books I was greatly in need of and therefore appropriated them. I am,

Very respectfully, your obedient servant,
G. M. Dodge,
Brigadier General.

The severe penalty of death, where a spy is captured, is not because there is anything dishonorable in the fact of the person being a spy, as only men of peculiar gifts for such service, men of courage and cool judgment and undoubted patriotism, are selected. The fact that the information they obtain is found within their enemy's lines, and the probability of great danger to an Army, is what causes the penalty to be so very severe. A soldier caught in the uniform, or a part of the uniform, of his enemy, within his enemy's lines, establishes the fact that he is a spy and is there in violation of the Articles of War and for no good purpose. This alone will prohibit his being treated as a prisoner of war, when caught, as Davis was, in our uniform, with valuable documents upon him, and seals his fate.

I appreciate fully that the people of Tennessee and Davis's comrades understand his soldierly qualities and propose to honor his memory. I take pleasure in aiding in raising the monument to his memory, although the services he performed were for the purpose of injuring my command, but given in faithfully performing the duties he was assigned to. I am

Truly and respectfully,
Grenville M. Dodge,
Major-General.

[Pg 171]

[Pg 172]

COMPANY L, FIFTY-FIRST IOWA INFANTRY, 1898, IN PHI-LIPPINES

Organized in 1856, as Council Bluffs Guards; Captain, G. M. Dodge; entered Civil War as Company B, Fourth Iowa Infantry. Now Company L, Fifty-first Iowa Infantry. Known locally as Dodge Light Guards.

[Pg 173]

GEN. G. M. DODGE ON THE "WATER CURE"

[The following is a reprint of an article that appeared originally in the New York Evening Post. —G. M. D.]

The New York Evening Post has thus been "called down" by General Grenville M. Dodge, who is well known throughout Iowa and the Nation as one of the leading Corps Commanders of the Union Army during the Civil War:

To the Editor of the Evening Post:

190

As one who has had some experience in the necessities, usages, and cruelties of war, which always prevail during a campaign in an enemy's country, I am surprised at the position of your journal, and its bitterness against the alleged action of Major Glenn, Lieutenant Conger, and Assistant Surgeon Lyon.

The testimony of Sergeant Riley, upon which you base your attack on these officers, goes to prove that they gave the water cure to a Filipino who had been made presidente in one of the provinces by our Government, who had taken the oath of allegiance to our country, and then used his official position to cover his acts as captain of an insurgent company which was acting in arms against our Army and within our lines. Therefore, he was a traitor and a spy, and his every act was a violation of the laws of war, and branded him an outlaw and guerilla. If these are the facts, under the usages of war these officers were justified in what they did; in fact, if they had shot the traitor they would never have been called to account, and in all probability this is what would have happened to him in the Civil War.

An officer has great latitude under such circumstances, and it is not safe or fair to condemn one for almost any act that detects a traitor and spy in arms against the Government which he has sworn to protect, and which has put him in a position of trust. You ignore entirely this side of the question, and only treat Major Glenn's acts as cruelties to peaceable Filipino citizens. I can remember when the journals of this country upheld and applauded an officer who, in the Civil War, ordered a man shot if he attempted to haul down the American flag, and cannot understand the present hysterics of some journals over the terrible violation of the laws of war in punishing a traitor, caught in the act, with the water cure only. The treatment may have been severe, but it is not permanently harmful.

I am astonished that these fearfully wrought-up journals have no word of commendation for our soldiers in the Philippines, who have suffered untold cruelties, assassinations, burning by slow fires, burial alive, mutilations, and atrocities; who have submitted to every indignity without resentment or complaint; and I have been greatly gratified over their excellent behavior under such trying circumstances. In their comments these journals are very careful not to say why these punishments are given to such traitors, knowing well if they did our people would look upon the acts as one of the necessities of war, and would wonder at the leniency of Major Glenn and his command.

Grenville M. Dodge.

New York, April 17.

[Pg 174] There can be no doubt that "war is hell," no matter whether it be on the Philippine Islands or any other place in the world. There has been much howling over the administration of "the water cure" in the Philippines, but every man who has had one year's experience in real war will admit that that "cure" is not so severe as killing or wounding captured enemies who have knowledge of hidden arms or other Army supplies. Every one of the "water-cured" Filipinos was given the opportunity to escape that punishment, but refused to tell what he knew and was therefore rightly punished until he was willing to tell the truth. General Dodge's letter proves that the punishment was justified, and his opinion will be sustained by every person who has knowledge of "the necessities, usages, and cruelties of war," which "always prevail during a campaign in an enemy's country." The truth is that the armies of the United States have been too lenient in the Philippines. That is the reason why the war has been so long continued, and the only reason why the final peace will be still further delayed. War is never a picnic, but should at all times be made terrible in order that peace and safety may be speedily gained. "The water cure" is inclined to be slightly irritating to the throats of the traitors in the Philippines, it is true, but it is not so bad or so cruel as maiming them for life, or killing them. The yellow journals may continue to howl, but the loyal American people will sustain the soldiers of the Nation in every effort to compel peace that comes within the rules of war.

[Pg 175]

[Pg 176]

SCOTTS BLUFFS

Major-General G. M. Dodge and train on march from Julesburg to Fort Laramie, in the Indian Campaign, August, 1865.

[Pg 177]

MISPLACED SYMPATHY

Address to The
New York Commandery, Military Order of Loyal
Legion, on Cruelties in the Philippines

I desire to enter my protest and call the attention of the companions to the position of a portion of the public press, and some people, towards our Army in the Philippines, and what they assert are cruelties perpetrated there.

There is a certain portion of the press, and also of the people, who are and always have been absolutely opposed to the operations of our army in the Philippines. They were very anxious to push us into a war which we were all opposed to, but after getting us there they refused to accept the results, and have persistently opposed everything done that was not in exact accordance with their views. In order to work upon the sympathies of the people, some of the papers are publishing pictures showing our soldiers in the very act of committing great outrages; the pictures were manufactured in their own offices, as were also most of the outrages complained of. You have not, however, seen in these papers any pictures portraying the cruelties perpetrated upon our soldiers, which have been worse than any acts ever committed by the savages in our wars with them; they are, in fact, too revolting to relate. I have had much to do with Indian warfare, but have never seen any cruelties to be compared with those inflicted upon our soldiers by the Filipinos, and these occurrences were not rare, but general,—happening all the time. Very little has been said on this subject, for it was not the policy of the Government to have the stories of these atrocities printed, or brought before the people; but now that our army is being so bitterly attacked, it is time that, the soldiers' side of the question should be presented, and we are learning of the soldiers who have been assassinated, their feet burned, buried alive, killed by slow-burning fires, their bowels cut open and wound around [Pg 178] trees. The Filipinos indulged in every torture and indignity that was possible, and, as a general thing, our soldiers did not retaliate. How they managed to refrain from taking vengeance is beyond my comprehension, but their action is greatly to their credit and honor.

The questions I wish to bring before you, however, are, What are the rights of an officer in such matters? What are his duties and privileges in war in an enemy's country that is under martial law? Take, for instance, General Smith's position when he was sent to Samar, with instructions to wipe out the insurrection there. He is said to have issued instructions to kill everybody found in arms that was over ten years of age, and to burn the country, if it was necessary to wipe out the insurrection, and the result is that in ninety days or less he did wipe out the insurrection, and without any great loss on our side or on the part of the enemy. Now they are denouncing him for a threat,—not an act. The temptation to retaliate must have been very great, for the treatment the Ninth Infantry received from those savages was nothing short of murder, followed by the most horrible mutilation, by a people who pretended to be their friends and at peace. In the ninety days he was operating there General Smith brought the island to peace, everybody in it had surrendered, and it is quiet. If he had made war under the methods advocated, allowing no one to be hurt, in all probability the subjugation of the island would have required a year's time, and there would have been ten times the suffering and loss of life than actually occurred. He simply followed the plan of war that was pursued by Grant, Sherman, and other commanders in the Civil War; that is, made it just as effective and short as possible. You know Sherman's position was that after a certain length of time when an enemy had been whipped, it was their duty to cease making war, and if they did not do so, he considered that any means were justifiable in order to bring it to an end. He stated this very clearly in his St. Louis speech. He stated the case as follows:

I claim that when we took Vicksburg, by all the rules of civilized warfare the Confederates should have surrendered, and allowed us to restore peace in the land. I claim also that when we took Atlanta they were bound by every rule of civilized warfare to surrender their cause, which was then hopeless, and it was clear as daylight that they were bound to surrender and return to civil life; but they continued the war, and then we had a right under the rules of civilized warfare to commence a system that would make them feel the power of the Government, and make them succumb. I had to go through Georgia to let them see what war meant. I had a right to destroy, which I did, and I made them feel the consequences of war so fully they will never again invite an invading Army.

[Pg 179] You all know of the troubles that occurred in the border states during the Civil War, and of the cruelties to the families of Union men who entered our Army. It was father against son, brother against brother, and, as General Sherman said, "It was cruelty, and there was no refining it." We know what severe orders were given for treatment of enemies within our lines, when their acts were in violation of the laws of war. In one case torpedoes were placed under a road over which our troops were marching, and several soldiers were killed. Sherman happened to come along just at that time, and said to the Colonel of the First Alabama Cavalry, which was his escort, "Burn the country within fifteen miles surrounding this spot." You all know what that meant; it was a license under which other things besides burning was done. An eyewitness describes Sherman's march to the sea and through the Carolinas as a "cloud of smoke by day and a pillar of fire by night." Who ever made the suggestion that Sherman's uniform should be stripped off for this, or that he should be shot, as some of our representatives in Congress and our press now demand should be done in the Philippines for making war in earnest?

Take another case, where Captain Anderson captured a train of convalescent unarmed Union soldiers in North Missouri, and placed them in line and shot every one of them. Shortly afterwards Colonel Johnson, of the Missouri State Militia, who was following Anderson, came up. Anderson attacked, this militia command of 160 men and killed 143, only seventeen getting away. Only one man was taken alive, and he saved himself by giving a Masonic sign. The war records are full of cases of individual acts, and I select one of which I had personal knowledge. It is found in volume 38, of the War Records. The orders in Missouri at that time were that any person who harbored a guerilla, and did not report the fact to the nearest commanding Union officer, should receive the same treatment as the guerilla. A man by the name of McReynolds violated these orders, and harbored Quantrell, the guerilla, and the officer who detected it, after stating all the facts and evidence, reported to me as follows:

On consultation with the squadron commanders, Captain Hamblin and Lieutenant Grain, it was decided to execute McReynolds, which was carried out under my orders.

R. M. Box.
Captain Company H, Seventh Cavalry, Missouri State Militia.

In reporting this case to the Adjutant General in Washington I did not approve it, as my investigation showed that the statements [Pg 180] of McReynolds's acts were true. I did not censure the officers, but issued an order that officers should follow more closely the orders of the Department, and ended that order as follows: "Hereafter men caught in arms will have no mercy shown them." General John McNeill, of Missouri, took twelve citizens out and shot them, it being claimed they were connected with guerillas that shot a Union man. In some histories it is known as the Palmyra massacre. It is claimed that the Union man turned up alive. If the reports of the numbers of robbers, guerillas and outlaws who were shot on sight in Kentucky, Missouri, Tennessee, and elsewhere, by both sides in 1864 and 1865, could be gathered up they would furnish retaliations and cruelties enough for these water-cure journals for years.

Consider this matter in a broader sense. Take the order of General Grant to General Sheridan to make the Shenandoah Valley a barren waste; it was absolutely destroyed so the enemy could not again occupy it. I can see no difference between an order to make the Shenandoah Valley a barren waste and Smith's order to make Samar a "howling wilderness." Take the order I received to go to the rear of Bragg's Army and destroy the Valley of the Tennessee, and all the supplies gathered there for the use of his Army, which valley was burned from Bear River to Decatur. These were orders from principal officers in our Army, and I only quote them to show the contrast between that time and the present. Senators in the halls of Congress find it necessary in these days to take up the question. Senator Rawlins, of Utah, made an attack upon our officers, and especially upon General Chaffee, which was nothing short of disgraceful, and should not be allowed to go without vigorous condemnation. He represents a state and people under whose orders Lieutenant Gunnison and his party were massacred by Mormons disguised as Indians. Some one should get up in the Senate and call him to account for these things, and ask him, in consideration of these facts, why he is so deeply outraged by the orders of General Chaffee, a gallant soldier and gentleman, a humane man, and one who, in my opinion, has done nothing in the Philippines but what was perfectly justified, and will in time be considered to have been humane.

The two Senators from Colorado have taken it upon themselves to denounce in bitter terms what they call unheard-of acts and cruelties of our Army. I would point them to a case in their [Pg 181] own state, which was more severe than any act in the Philippines has been. A regiment of Colorado cavalry under Colonel J. M. Chivington, a minister by profession, attacked and destroyed a band of Indians encamped on the Big Sandy, near Camp Lyon, who claimed to be under the protection of the officers at Fort Lyon. This was a massacre of men, women and children of a friendly band of Indians, and was one of the main causes of bringing into arms against the United States every tribe of Indians south of the Yellowstone. When an investigation of this affair was ordered the State of Colorado almost unanimously protested against it, upholding the act, and quoted that old saying, "There is no good Indian except a dead one." Think of our wars with the Indians in which whole bands were wiped out, even the women and children being destroyed; think of the wars in which we employed Indians against Indians; they not only killed but scalped. I do not know of a single treaty ever made with the Indians that the United States has not violated, and when an Indian had the hardihood to object the Government started in to wipe him out. This has been the treatment of the Indians from the Atlantic to the Pacific, until at the present time there is not a wild Indian living in the entire country; yet I cannot remember that this press has ever been aroused; it was too near home.

Take the case of Major Glenn, who is about to be courtmartialed for giving the water cure to the presidente in one of the Provinces of Luzon, as the testimony goes to show. This presidente had been appointed to office by our Government, had taken the oath of allegiance, and was there to represent us. While he was occupying this position, it was discovered that he was the captain of an insurgent company, giving active assistance to the enemy, and he was, therefore, a traitor and a spy, and under the laws of war deserved to be shot; but instead they proposed to courtmartial Glenn for simply giving him the water cure; and this, in my opinion, is a great wrong.

Order 100, which is often quoted, was issued in the Civil War to govern officers. It was prepared by Professor Lieber, and was considered and adopted, I believe, by a board of officers; anyhow, it was very carefully drawn. I am told it has been considered and used by nearly all the nations. It gives an officer great latitude, and where an officer meets a savage enemy, or one that is violating the laws of war, those laws are suspended and it virtually is left [Pg 182] to his own judgment as to how far he should go in inflicting punishment, and under this order there is no doubt both Smith and Glenn were protected in their actions. It may seem harsh, but you are all aware how many harsh orders were given in the Civil War for the purpose of forcing the enemy to obey our orders, and how often those orders and threats accomplished the purpose without any other act. When the colored troops were first organized, on several occasions Confederate officers sent in demands for them to surrender, coupled with the threat that if they refused the place would be taken and no quarter granted. I know of one instance where an officer believed this threat and surrendered a Regiment of colored infantry for the purpose of having them protected. Then there is the case of Fort Pillow; whether or not Forest gave the order it is claimed he gave, I do not know; but the fact that no quarter was shown there has been amply verified.

Within the past week there has been appointed a committee of distinguished citizens, most of whom are well-known opponents of our Government in its policies and acts during the Spanish War. They propose to hunt up and lay before Congress all cases of cruelty on the part of our Army, with the avowed purpose of sustaining the national honor. I must say this is the first time I ever heard of national honor being sustained by such methods. Have you, or any one else, ever heard a single word of protest from these people or any one connected with them against the revolting cruelties of the enemy in the Philippines? They evidently have no desire to learn about these things, but want some excuse for attacking our Army, hoping thereby to bring dishonor upon our country before the world. The national honor never has, never can, and never will be protected by such methods. It is upheld and maintained today, as it always has been, by the patriotism of our people as represented by our Army in the Civil War, in Cuba, the Philippines, and China.

These attacks upon the Army are for a double purpose, and you should not forget it. Every time they make this great hubbub about cruelties they are hitting back at those that were in the Civil War. There is an element in this country that already has no use for the soldier of the Civil War. They are continually crying about the pension he is getting; that he is favored in the Government service; etc., etc. They do not dare attack him openly, as yet, but do it covertly. There is no officer listening to me who [Pg 183] did not see cruelties in the Civil War. Many of you have had to order them, but you know you were never brought to account for them when they were acts of necessity. We were always careful that no cruelties were committed by enlisted men, but whatever was done was by the order of an officer. It was the practice of the War Department never to interfere in these matters, leaving them to the officer who was in charge of the forces in the field. None of these things occurred without his knowledge; he was on the spot and knew the necessity for them, and if he did not take action it was considered that none was necessary, and they were seldom called to account for it afterwards; but in the Philippines they are bringing officers to account simply because of the outcry of people who care nothing for the merits of the case, except to make capital against our country's policy in maintaining itself in the Philippines. In view of all the facts, I must doubt the sincerity of those who are seeking to bring discredit upon our little Army, the marvellous efficiency of which has won the admiration of the world. Under the regulations, it is impossible for the Army to defend itself and make answer to these attacks, except through their own officers, and their reports do not reach the public, for the press seems to use only that which reflects upon the Army, and omits that which is in its favor. It is the duty of every companion here, as well as of every good citizen, to enter his protest against these unjust attacks. The right side is beginning to get a hearing, and when the facts and causes for the action of the Army are generally known, it will be found that our Army is as humane and well-behaved a body of troops as ever went into a foreign country, and we must all assist in seeing that it receives justice.